POSTMODERNISM, REASON AND RELIGION

On questions of faith, Ernest Gellner believes, three ideological options are available to us today. One is the return to a genuine and firm faith in a religious tradition. The other is a form of relativism which abandons the notion of unique truth altogether, and resigns itself to treating truth as relative to the society or culture in question. The third, which Gellner calls enlightenment rationalism, upholds the idea that there *is* a unique truth, but denies that any society can ever possess it definitively.

The first option – religious fundamentalism – is particularly strong in Muslim societies, and Gellner investigates why this is so. He finds the explanation in the relationship between high culture and low culture within Islam, where the high culture, previously the achievement of the minority, has now become the pervasive culture of the entire society. This high culture, within Muslim societies, performs a function very similar to that performed by nationalisms elsewhere. The second option – relativism – is exemplified in the west by the postmodernist movement. Gellner is highly critical of postmodernism, arguing that it indulges in subjectivism as a form of expiation for the sins of colonialism. The objectivity pursued as an ideal by social science during the colonial period was in fact a tool of domination, and subjectivist relativism is a way of freeing ourselves from that. Gellner explores the strengths and weaknesses of the third option, the option he prefers, arguing that this works only on assumption of inner compromise, and a separation of truth taken seriously from truth used as a kind of cultural decoration.

Learned and stimulating, Professor Gellner's book is an important contribution to our understanding of postmodernism and the relations between Islam and the West. It will be of great interest to anyone concerned with the ideological condition of contemporary society.

POSTMODERNISM, REASON AND RELIGION

Ernest Gellner

London and New York

First published in 1992
by Routledge
11 New Fetter Lane, London EC4P 4EE

Simultaneously published in the USA and Canada
by Routledge
a division of Routledge, Chapman and Hall Inc.
29 West 35th Street, New York, NY 10001

© 1992 Ernest Gellner

Phototypeset in Palatino by Intype, London
Printed and bound in Great Britain by Richard Clay Ltd, Bungay, Suffolk

British Library Cataloguing in Publication Data
A catalogue record for this book is available from the British Library.

Library of Congress Cataloging in Publication Data
Gellner, Ernest.
Postmodernism, reason and religion / Ernest Gellner.
p. cm.
Includes bibliographical references and index.
1. Postmodernism—Religious aspects. I. Title.
BL65.P73G45 1992
291.2—dc20   91–43166
                                                    CIP

ISBN 0–415–08024–X

CONTENTS

PREFACE   vii

POSTMODERNISM, REASON AND RELIGION   1

Religious Fundamentalism   2

Postmodernism and Relativism   22

Relativismus über Alles   40

The Characters   72

The Third Man   75

Rationalist Fundamentalism   80

NOTES   97

INDEX   101

PREFACE

This book was originally written as a text which was to constitute *one half* of a larger volume, the other half to be written
by a serious believing and practising Muslim, Professor Akbar
Ahmed, with whose work I have long been familiar, given a
shared interest in Muslim tribal organization. The invitation
had come from Professor Ahmed and was confirmed by the
publishers, and the book was written in conformity with the
requirements of a contract which envisaged such a composite
volume.

I accepted the invitation for various reasons, which included
the consideration that it was a good thing to show that a full-
blooded, committed believer and an intellectual adherent of
Enlightenment doubt could face each other within the compass
of a single volume, discussing, more or less, the same theme,
and to do so with courtesy and in an amicable manner. It
might even set a good example.

In my argument, my intention was to describe and analyse
the triangular situation which arises in the contemporary
world, with three basic positions: fundamentalism, which
believes in a unique truth and which believes itself to be in
possession of it; relativism, in a variety of formulations, which
forswears the idea of a unique truth, but tries to treat each
particular vision as if it were none the less true; and a position
of which I am more or less an adherent, which retains the
faith in the uniqueness of truth, but does not believe we ever
possess it definitively, and which uses, as the foundation for

vii

practical conduct and inquiry, not any substantive conviction, but only a loyalty to certain procedural rules.

These seem to be the three principal contestants for our intellectual loyalty, and if representatives of two of them, with very different backgrounds, could meet in one volume, it might be a good thing. I know, or think I know, roughly what Professor Ahmed's position is; I did not read his text, and did not encourage him to read mine, for that might set off a kind of unending regress of mutual interaction.

When the texts reached the publishers, they decided that they preferred to publish them separately. Ahmed and I both accepted this decision, though the terms of reference under which our texts had been written had been different from this. I have no strong feelings about the precise form in which my thoughts reach whatever public they do reach: they remain, after all, the same thoughts. Nevertheless, I do wish to say all this about the origin of this text, for it will explain to the reader some features of the presentation of the ideas, which would in all probability have been different, had I known that I was simply writing a book, rather than one half of a co-operative book. It is not that I would have said something different, but I might well have said it differently, at least in some measure. Readers eager to see both stories may still read both books (see Akbar S. Ahmed, *Postmodernism and Islam*, London: Routledge, 1992).

Whilst working on the text, I received invaluable help and moral support from the staff of the Social Anthropology Department (Cambridge) office, which at that time consisted of Mrs Mary McGinley, Mrs Margaret Story, Mrs Anne Farmer and Mr Humphrey Hinton. I received additional and most effective help from Miss Sarah Green. My son David read an earlier version and as usual made very useful suggestions which in the main I adopted. I was able to secure technical aids thanks to grants from both the Economic and Social Research Council and the Nuffield Foundation. Thanks are also due to Justin Dyer, who copy-edited the typescript. I feel much indebted to all those mentioned, and also to some who are not. Given the possibly touchy nature of some of the themes handled, it is as well to restate that the views expressed, for what they are worth, are mine alone.

Ernest Gellner

POSTMODERNISM, REASON AND RELIGION

There is a tendency for the major intellectual conflicts in human history to be binary. Great issues polarize mankind. In the Wars of Religion, Catholics faced Protestants; later, it was Faith which confronted Reason. During more recent times, liberalism competed with socialism. Minor schismatics would of course make alliances across the great divide; political opportunism will lead to the oddest liaisons, and, tactically, both doctrinal and political alignments might be very complex. But all in all, one central issue tended to dominate the situation.

On questions of faith, however, our contemporary scene seems to have ceased to be binary. There are not two, but three basic contestants. There are three fundamental and irreducible positions. Three primary colours are required for mapping our condition. It would be quite wrong to try to reduce any one of them to a mere extreme exaggeration or modification of any one of the others, or to see it as a compromise version of the two others. Each expresses a fundamental option of the human spirit, when facing the world as it is now.

The three great positions seem to be roughly equidistant from each other. Thus a rather symmetrical situation arises. Any pair of the three has some features in common, but not to the extent of creating a special and predominant affinity, or a specially potent revulsion, between them. As in Sartre's *Huis Clos*, the tense situation is rather evenly balanced and

1

inherently unstable. None of the possible links is more natural and more persistent than the others. Alliances crystallize, but their internal strains and inescapable disappointment inevitably provoke re-alignments, and no participant can really settle down in a stable liaison. It is all somewhat like the children's game of scissors, paper and rock: the scissors cut paper, the paper wraps the rock, the rock blunts the scissors. There is no stable dominance, only inherent instability.

What are the three contestants?

1 Religious fundamentalism.
2 Relativism, exemplified for instance by the recent fashion of 'postmodernism'.
3 Enlightenment rationalism, or rationalist fundamentalism.

The three expressions are used without prejudice: the names are simply code terms. They are not intended in themselves to decide any issues. What is read into those terms will emerge only in the course of the discussion.

RELIGIOUS FUNDAMENTALISM

The idea or position associated with this term is clear. Rigorism, or, in French, 'intégrisme', also provides suggestive names for the same phenomenon. The underlying idea is that a given faith is to be upheld firmly in its full and literal form, free of compromise, softening, re-interpretation or diminution. It presupposes that the core of religion is *doctrine*, rather than ritual, and also that this doctrine can be fixed with precision and finality, which further presupposes *writing*.

Fundamentalism is best understood in terms of what it repudiates. It rejects the widespread modern idea that religion, though endowed with some kind of nebulously specified validity of its own, really doesn't mean what it actually says, and least of all what ordinary people had in the past naturally taken it to mean. What it really means, according to such repudiated modernism, is something quite other – something which turns out to be radically different from what its unsophisticated adherents had previously taken it to mean, and some-

2

thing far removed from the natural interpretation of the claims of the faith in question. Fundamentalism repudiates the tolerant modernist claim that the faith in question means something much milder, far less exclusive, altogether less demanding and much more accommodating; above all something quite compatible with all other faiths, even, or especially, with the lack of faith. Such modernism extracts all demand, challenge and defiance from the doctrine and its revelation.

One major source of this tradition is the famous nineteenth-century Danish theologian and writer Søren Kierkegaard. He is associated with the idea that religion is of its essence not persuasion of the truth of a doctrine, but *commitment* to a position which is inherently absurd, which, to use his own term, gives *offence*.[1] We attain our identity, he says, by believing something that deeply offends our mind. This makes it sound very, very difficult. To *exist*, we must believe, and believe something dreadfully hard to believe. You cannot come to exist by just believing something plausible. This is the existentialist twist which links faith to identity rather than evidence.

But beware: underneath the seemingly stern demand, there is a warrant for great facility. If this is what religion is, if *commitment* is at issue, and all commitments are alike, there's no further need to be really troubled by any logical difficulties attaching to the content of that to which one is committed. To be troubled would be to show that one has mistaken commitment to an identity for assent to a demonstration (which it cannot be). So all's well, and all strain evaporates from the situation. That is a characteristically modernist position.

But there are many other variants. Faith can be seen, not so much as commitment, as the celebration of community. Affirmation of the supernatural is de-coded as expression of loyalty to a social order and its values. The doctrine de-coded along these lines is no longer haunted by doubt – for there isn't really any doctrine, only a *membership*, which for some reason employs doctrinal formulation as its token.

The cosmogony of a given faith, in such softened modernist re-interpretations, is in effect treated not as literal truth, but merely as some kind of parable, conveying 'symbolic' truths, something not to be taken at face value, and hence no longer liable to be in any kind of conflict with scientific pronouncements about what would, on the surface, seem to be the same topic. For instance, 'modernist' believers are untroubled by the incompatibility between the Book of Genesis and either Darwinism or modern astro-physics. They assume that the pronouncements, though seemingly about the same events – the creation of the world and the origins of man – are really on quite different levels, or even, as some would have it, in altogether different languages, within distinct or separate kinds of 'discourse'. Generally speaking, the doctrines and moral demands of the faith are then turned into something which, properly interpreted, is in astonishingly little conflict with the secular wisdom of the age, or indeed with anything. This way lies peace – and doctrinal vacuity.

Fundamentalism firmly repudiates this kind of watering down of the religious claims. Fundamentalism occurs in many religions, though not with the same vigour. In our age, fundamentalism is at its strongest in Islam. For this reason, the argument focuses on Islam.

The realm of Islam presents an interesting picture in the modern world. Sociologists have long entertained, and frequently endorsed, the theory of secularization. It runs as follows: the scientific-industrial society, religious faith and observance decline. One can give intellectualist reasons for this: the doctrines of religion are in conflict with those of science, which in turn are endowed with enormous prestige, and which constitute the basis of modern technology, and thereby also of modern economy. Therefore, religious faith declines. Its prestige goes down as the prestige of its rival rises.

Alternatively, one may give structural reasons: religion is linked to the celebration of the community, and in the atomized world of modern mass society, there is little community to celebrate, other than possibly the national state – and that state has found its own new ritual and set of values in nationalism. So the erosion of community life is reflected in the loss of faith, and the diminished appeal of ritual.

There are many variants of this theory. What matters is that, by and large, the secularization thesis does hold. Some political regimes are overtly associated with secularist, anti-religious ideologies; others are officially dissociated from religion, and practise secularism more by default than by active affirmation. But few states are formally associated with religion, or if they are, the link is loose, and not taken too seriously. Religious observance and participation are low. When they are higher, the content of the religion is often visibly social rather than transcendent: formal doctrine is ignored, and participation treated as a celebration of community not of conviction. Religious issues are seldom prominent. Where community survives, it seems to prefer to celebrate itself almost directly, without seeing itself through the prism of faith.

During the age of emergence of the world religions, stress shifted from lived ritual to transcendent doctrine, and it looks as if now the wheel has come full circle, and that where religion contains some vigour, it does so by becoming civic once again. In North America, religious attendance is high, but religion celebrates a shared cult of the American way of life, rather than insisting on distinctions of theology or church organization, as once it did.[2] Apparent exceptions to the trend towards secularization turn out on examination to be special cases, explicable by special circumstances, as when a church is used as a counter-organization against an oppressive state committed to a secular belief-system. It is possible to disagree about the extent, homogeneity or irreversibility of this trend,[3] and, unquestionably, secularization does assume many quite different forms; but, by and large, it would seem reasonable to say that it is real.

But there is one very real, dramatic and conspicuous exception to all this: Islam. To say that secularization prevails in Islam is not contentious. It is simply false. Islam is as strong now as it was a century ago. In some ways, it is probably much stronger.[4]

At the end of the Middle Ages, the Old World contained

four major civilizations. Of these, three are now, in one measure or another, secularized. Christian doctrine is bowdlerized by its own theologians, and deep, literal conviction is not conspicuous by its presence.[5] In the Sinic World, a secular faith has become formally established and its religious predecessors disavowed. In the Indian World, a state and the élite are neutral *vis-à-vis* what is a pervasive folk religion, even if practices such as astrology continue to be widespread. But in one of the four civilizations, the Islamic, the situation is altogether different.

Why should one particular religion be so markedly secularization-resistant? This is an important question. Whether the answer which will be offered is the correct one, I do not know, and I doubt whether anyone else does either: historical interpretations are difficult to establish. It happens to be the best I can offer; it may provide some illumination, whether or not it contains all the truth. If it provokes a better alternative theory, I shall be well satisfied.

Islam is a founded religion, claiming to complete and round off the Abrahamic tradition and its Prophets, and to do so with finality. Muhammad is the *Seal* of the Prophets. Earlier versions of the divine revelation, in the keeping of the two Abrahamic religions, are held by Muslims to have become distorted by their adherents.

The faith is based on the divine Message received by the Prophet Muhammad in the seventh century. The events which occurred during the first few generations of Muslims are recorded and vividly present to the consciousness of Muslims, and provide the basis for the division of Islam into three sects: the majoritarian Sunnis, the Shi'ites and the Kharejites. The Kharejites are the least numerous.

The central doctrines of Islam contain an emphatic and severe monotheism,[6] the view that the Message received by the Prophet is so to speak terminal, and that it contains both faith and morals – or, in other words, it is both doctrine and law, and that no genuine further augmentation is to be countenanced. The points of doctrine and points of law are not separated, and Muslim learned scholars are best described as theologians/jurists. There is no canon law, but simply divine law as such, applicable to the community of believers, rather than to the organization and members of some specialized agency.

The fact that, in this way, legislation is pre-empted by the deity has profound implications for Muslim life. It does not merely mean that a fundamentalist may have difficulties in accepting modern law and legislative practices; it also means that a certain kind of separation of powers was built into Muslim society from the very start, or very nearly from the start. This version of the separation of powers did not need to wait for some Enlightenment doctrine concerning the desirability of a pluralist social order and of the internal balance of independent institutions. It subordinates the executive to the (divine) legislature and, in actual practice, turns the theologians/lawyers into the monitors of political rectitude – whether or not they always have the power to enforce their verdicts.[7] The principle that 'the community will not agree on error' may endow communal consensus, rather than the political centre, with a kind of legislative authority. Within this communal consensus, the voice of the learned is liable to possess special weight. After all, the community must heed an already existing law and it is natural to respect the opinion of those better informed.

So, once the idea of a final and divine law came to be accepted, a law which in principle was to receive no further divine additions, and not to allow any human ones, the (human) executive became in the very nature of things distinct from the (divine, but communally mediated) legislative arm of government. Law could be extended at best by analogy and interpretation. Society was thus endowed with both a fundamental and concrete law, each in its way entrenched, and usable by its members as a yardstick of legitimate government. Entrenched constitutional law was, as it were, waiting and ever-ready for all polities. A socially and politically transcendent standard of rectitude was ever accessible, beyond the reach of manipulation by political authority, and available for condemning the *de facto* authority if it sinned against it. It only needed for that standard to possess an earthly ally, endowed with armed might, for the sinning authority – if it was held to be sinful – to be in trouble. The political history of Islam does display the periodic emergence of such a daunting alliance of transcendent rectitude and earthly might.[8]

Another striking and important feature of Islam is the theoretical absence of clergy. No distinct sacramental status separates the preacher or the leader of the ritual from the laity. Such a person is naturally expected to be more competent, above all in learning, but he is not a different kind of social being. Formally, there is no clerical organization. Muslim theology is in this sense egalitarian. Believers are equidistant from God.

There is no need to debate here whether in fact Islam really emerged complete at its very inception. Historically this is not a very plausible theory,[9] though Muslims may be committed to the idea that the Prophet and His Companions provided an immediate, permanent and valid model for the later community. It is an issue on which 'outside' historians and Muslims may disagree. But the issue is not relevant for the present purpose. What is relevant is that, eventually, a fairly homogeneous Muslim civilization did emerge, endowed with a clearly defined ideal and self-image.

The three central, pervasive and actually invoked principles of religious and political legitimacy within it are: the divine Message and its legal elaboration, the consensus of the community, and, finally, sacred leadership (by members of the House of the Prophet, or by specially selected members of it). It is the difference of relative stress on these three principles which separates the sects. Shi'ites (subdivided further) revere divine leaders, who are usually, but not in all cases, in 'occultation', in hiding in this world or another, and due to return from it at some unspecified future date; Kharejites are the most egalitarian and 'puritan' of the sects; whilst the Sunnites represent a central compromise with a heavy stress on the 'Sunna', i.e. corpus of the original revelation plus scholarly elaboration, and with a relatively mild insistence on the political privileges of the members of the House of the Prophet.[10]

Islam knew rapid and early political success, which is perhaps one of the reasons why a church/state dualism never emerged in it: the original charismatic community had no need to define itself as against a state which still remained alien. It *was* the state from the very start.

The turbulent early history of the community gave rise to the sectarian schisms. The Caliphate was, however, established, and it was in the course of the Ummayad and Abbasid dynasties that Islam assumed something like its present form. The Caliphate declined and collapsed by the thirteenth century, but Islam continued to be strong under a variety of succession states. An important fact is that the attempt by philosophically oriented scholars to inject a strong dose of pre-Islamic, Greek philosophy failed: it was the anti-philosophical theologians who prevailed. By the time of the great expansion of the Christian West, there were three very major Muslim states – the Ottoman, Persian and Mogul – plus a number of other, more peripheral ones.

Leaving aside the sectarian schism, the really central, and perhaps most important, feature of Islam is that it was internally divided into a High Islam of the scholars and the Low Islam of the people. The boundary between the two was not sharp, but was often very gradual and ambiguous, resembling in this respect the related but not identical line of demarcation between territories governed effectively from the political centre and territory governed by local tribes and their leaders. Muslim states, however autocratic in theory, in practice had to accommodate themselves to the local autonomy of self-administering tribes.

It was the alliance of such tribes, temporarily united by enthusiasm for divine law brought to them by an inspired and revered preacher, which constituted the permanent menace to the existing state. So their absolutism of the polity was in fact limited, on the one side, by the actual power of tribes, and, on the other, by the independent and un-manipulable legitimacy of divine law. The danger for the Muslim ruler was the fusion of these two forces: a revivalist movement insisting on the maintenance or restoration of uncompromising religious truth, and sustained by the support of cohesive, armed and militarily experienced rural self-governing communities. These communities *normally* practised a culturally 'low' variant of the faith, but were eager to embrace the purer, unitarian 'high' form under the influence of a wave of enthusiasm, and in hope of urban booty and political privilege.

The difference between High and Low Islam was not only gradual, but it was also often obscured, and barely perceived. This ambiguity or obscurity, the fact that the distinction could often be ignored, and that it did *not* congeal into a recognized boundary, was a very essential feature of the situation. The difference was expressed in a *de facto* diversity of ritual style, but it did not become externalized and public as an overt sectarian schism. The difference between the two styles would be politely ignored, and their practitioners could co-exist amicably. The adherents of the low form could even revere the higher form and recognize its authority, whilst continuing to indulge in the lower variant. Confrontation would be avoided.

At times, however, the latent tension between the two styles re-emerged, and, periodically, High Islam would launch a kind of internal purification movement, and attempt to re-impose itself on the whole of society. In the long term they were never successful, so that the resulting pattern was one of what might be called an eternal or cyclical reformation. Ibn Khaldun noted this pattern,[11] as did David Hume.[12] Friedrich Engels also commented on it,[13] remarking on the fact that whilst in both Christianity and Islam the idiom of political struggle was religious, in Christianity it led to a real change, whereas in Islam it merely led to a repetition and a rotation of personnel in an unchanging social order. Engels was almost certainly influenced by Ibn Khaldun, though he does not quote him by name.

Engels was evidently rather disdainful of this as it were cyclical stagnation of the Orientals, Muslims most specially, and did not seem bothered by the fact that he was thereby contradicting one of the central and indispensable tenets of Marxism – the view that all class-endowed societies must be inherently unstable, and that their 'contradictions' would make genuine permanence and perpetuation of class domination impossible.[14] Progress, tension and the dialectic were, it would appear, a Western prerogative, and the East could be consigned to a stagnation from which only the West could liberate it.

What is the difference between the two religious styles? High Islam is carried by urban scholars, recruited largely from the trading bourgeoisie (which often combines scholarship with trade), and reflects the natural tastes and values of urban middle classes (at least if one thinks primarily of Edinburgh, Geneva, Fez or Amsterdam, rather than of Venice, Florence or Kathmandu). Those values include order, rule-observance, sobriety, learning. They contain an aversion to hysteria and emotional excess, and to the excessive use of the audio-visual aids of religion. This High Islam stresses the severely monotheistic and nomocratic nature of Islam, it is mindful of the prohibition of claims to mediation between God and man, and it is generally oriented towards puritanism and scripturalism.[15]

Low Islam, or Folk Islam, is different. If it knows literacy, it does so mainly in the use of writing for magical purposes, rather than as a tool of scholarship. It stresses magic more than learning, ecstacy more than rule-observance. Rustics, you might say, encounter writing mainly in the form of amulets, manipulative magic and false land deeds. Far from avoiding mediation, this form of Islam is centred on it: its most characteristic institution is the saint cult, where the saint is more often than not a living rather than a dead personage (and where sanctity is transmitted from father to son). This form of the faith is most visible through those loose associations of ranked saints and saint-centres, generally known in the literature as religious brotherhoods, Orders or fraternities.

Each of these two religious styles has its place in the social structure. Saint cults are prominent in the tribal or semi-tribal countryside, and provide invaluable services in the semi-anarchic rural conditions: mediation between groups, facilitation of trade by associating it with pilgrimage, and, last but not least, provision of the symbolism by means of which illiterate rustic believers can identify enthusiastically with a scriptural religion. Rural Muslims may be 'bad' Muslims by the standards of urban scholarship, and they know it, but their reverence for local saints supposedly linked to the Prophet by genealogy, and to urban ideals though alleged feats of scholarship by the saint's ancestors, enables them to identify wholeheartedly and passionately with the central religious tradition.

Saint cults also provide services for the urban poor, whom they provide with ecstatic superrogatory rituals, better fitted to provide escape from a miserable condition than the more austere orthodoxy. Mystical exercises provide better consolation for deprivation than does scholastic theology and casuistic jurisprudence. If opium is indeed required for the people, then ecstatic mysticism serves better than scholastic theology and legal casuistry. The saints also provide therapeutic services, and, generally speaking, it is hard not to see them as a kind of surrogate clergy in a formally clergy-less faith.

The educationally and economically more privileged urban strata certainly hold up their noses at some of the wilder practices of the saints and their followers,[16] the snake-charming, drug use, hysteria, possession, dancing, and so forth; but it would be quite wrong to think that in normal times they abstain from these saint-led religious practices altogether. 'He who has no sheikh has the devil for his sheikh', went a Moroccan saying (where sheikh here means a leader of a religious order). Equally, it would be wrong to think of the lower orders and rural populations being uncritically devoted to the saints they habitually use: 'There is always a snake in a zawiya', goes the Algerian saying, where zawiya is a saintly centre.[17] Rustics use saints, revere them, and joke about them.

High Islam provides the urban population, and to some extent the whole society, with its charter and its entrenched constitution, in the name of which they can protest against excesses, notably undue taxation, by the state. The urban mob can riot under the leadership of a respected scholar, but this is not too grave a danger for the established authorities: the real danger for them lies in the alliance between a respected scholar and the militarily formidable peripheral tribes. Ironically, it is these tribes, whose daily practices and knowledge of religion, from the viewpoint of urban orthodoxy, leave much to be desired, who also provided the sword-arm which, from time to time, endowed that same orthodoxy with military and political clout, and made possible a great renewal. The preacher unites a group of tribes, upbraids them for their own ignorance and laxity, but at the same time urges them to support him in cleaning up the corruption in the city and its court, which incidentally means booty for *them*. If Paris is worth a Mass, then the tribesman generally reckoned that Fez (or some similar city) is worth a bit of purity. It is in this form that the circulation of élites operated in traditional Islam.

This pattern of state-formation or dynasty-initiation occurred quite frequently, well into modern times. Some of these movements occurred just a little too early to be explained in terms of the impact of the West: the Wahabi movement in central Arabia, Osman dan Fodio's jihad in Northern Nigeria, the Sanussiyya in Cyrenaica, the Mahdia in the Sudan. Others were clearly reactions to Western expansion: Abd el Kader in Algeria, Abd el Krim in Northern Morocco, the 'Mad Mullah' in Somaliland, Shamil in the Caucasus. The Wahabi movement and that of Osman dan Fodio continue to this day to be the foundations of the political order in their respective countries. The movements vary in the extent to which they are based exclusively on the principles of High Islam: its ideas often tend to be present, but the need for organization can also oblige it to adopt the terminology and organization principles of the religious Orders. The Sanusiyya used the organizational principles of an Order to propogate revivalist ideas.

What happened to these movements in the past, and what happens to them in the modern world? The coming of the modern world has made an enormous difference. In the traditional world, as Ibn Khaldun, and Friedrich Engels echoing him, had noted, the wheel simply turned full circle. The reformers prevailed (not all of them of course – many are called but few are chosen – but a few of them did, from time to time), and, having re-established a purified order, things slowly returned to normality. The spirit is willing but the social flesh is weak. Literate, rule-abiding scripturalist puritanism is

13

practicable for urban scholars, but not so for the mass, or for the rural tribesmen. They may embrace it during the ardent period of revival and the struggle for its enforcement, but they will forget it when they return to the home life of camp and village. For reasons well explored by Durkheimian sociology, they need a form of religion which provides society with its temporal and spatial markers, which indicates the boundaries of sub-groups and of seasonal activities, and which provides the rituals and the masters of ceremonies for the festivals which endow life with its pattern.[18] The social structure has its reasons of which the theological mind knows nothing. And so the rival style of faith re-affirms itself, often under the aegis of the successors and offspring of the very reformers who had ridden to power under the banners of reforming zeal.

But under modern conditions, this no longer happens.[19] The old status quo was based on a military and political balance of power, in which the central authority simply lacked the means to assert itself effectively in the desert and in the mountains, and, in a large part of the countryside, left the maintenance of order to self-administering local groups, normally known as 'tribes'. The urgent need for mediation between local social segments, the requirement of orchestration of the rhythm of social life, called forth those mediators – conductors of the balance of power and of the festivals, known as saints. They came back as quickly as they were purged.

But all this has now changed. The administrative, transport, communication and military technology available to the colonial and post-colonial state leads to effective unification, and in most cases (though there are some exceptions such as North Yemen) to effective political centralization, and so to the erosion of the erstwhile local mutual-aid groups. Their weakening means the disappearance, or radical diminution, of the need for the services of their habitual mediators. Like the French aristocracy during the final stages of the *ancien régime*, according to Tocqueville, the saints find themselves still endowed with their privileges, but no longer with their functions, a situation well calculated to call forth resentment. And so it is: suddenly, the believers remember that their more reputable version of the faith proscribes mediation, or they listen to preachers most eager to remind them of it. Renewal of the true version of the faith returns with a vengeance, and, this time, it returns for good.

Islam, having in the past been an eternal or cyclical reformation, ever reforming the morals of the faithful, but never doing so for good, turned in the course of the past hundred years into a definitive and, as far as one can judge, irreversible reformation. There has been an enormous shift in the balance *from* Folk Islam *to* High Islam. The social bases of Folk Islam have been in large part eroded, whilst those of High Islam were greatly strengthened. Urbanization, political centralization, incorporation in a wider market, labour migration, have all impelled populations in the direction of the formally (theologically) more 'correct' Islam.

Identification with Reformed Islam has played a role very similar to that played by nationalism elsewhere. In Muslim countries, it is indeed difficult to distinguish the two movements. The average believer can hardly continue to identify with his local tribe or shrine. The tribe has fallen apart, the shrine is abandoned. By modern standards, both are suspect, a good piece of folklore for tourists, but a little beneath the dignity of an urbanized citizen of a modern state. The city-dweller does not display himself in public at the shrine festival, and still less does he allow his wife, daughter or sister to do so. He does not settle his disputes by calling his cousins to defend or to testify at a shrine, he knows the feud is proscribed and will be suppressed by the police; he knows he can better protect himself by using whatever pull he may have in the official and informal political networks.

Islam provides a national identity, notably in the context of the struggle with colonialism – the modern Muslim 'nation' is often simply the sum-total of Muslims on a given territory. Reformist Islam confers a genuine shared identity on what would otherwise be a mere summation of the under-privileged. It also provides a kind of ratification of the social ascension of many contemporary Muslims, from rustic status to becoming better-informed town-dwellers, or at least town-oriented persons.

Contrary to what outsiders generally suppose, the typical Muslim woman in a Muslim city doesn't wear the veil because her grandmother did so, but because her grandmother did *not*: her grandmother in her village was far too busy in the fields, and she frequented the shrine without a veil, and left the veil to her betters. The granddaughter is celebrating the fact that she has joined her grandmother's betters, rather than her loyalty to her grandmother. Islam also continues to perform its old role of a kind of eternal entrenched constitution, by means of which the now rather expanded bourgeoisie can criticize, and perhaps on occasion check, the technocratic mamluks at the top. When the mamluks become persuaded to introduce genuine elections (by the desire to implement internationally respected norms of political practice, say), they are liable to find themselves replaced at the voting booths not by populists, but by fundamentalists.

All this, as far as I can see, is the mechanism responsible for a very major cultural revolution which took place in the world of Islam in the course of the past century, a revolution barely noticed, at least until very recently, by the West. The West has come to perceive that something big is happening mainly under the impact of the Iranian cataclysm, but this calls for some special comments. Shi'ism is somewhat untypical within Islam, and, though it does fit the overall diagnosis offered, qualifications are required. Shi'ism has some of the features characteristic of Folk Islam within Sunnism, notably the very important tendency towards a cult of personality: Shi'ism is virtually definable in terms of reverence for, and attribution of ultimate political and theological sovereignty to, the 'Hidden Imam'. The situation is complicated by the fact that this divine personage is generally in hiding, so that in the meanwhile, pending his return, the tasks of political and religious administration must needs be undertaken by someone else. One is tempted to say that those very psychic or social forces which in later centuries led Muslims towards saint-worship (but which then no longer led, in most cases, to schism), had led, during the early, inchoate stage of the crystallization of faith, to the Shi'ite secession, inspired by devotion to sacred leaders and martyrs.

But if what makes Islam so acceptable in the modern world is its puritanical, egalitarian, scripturalist face, why has its greatest, most dramatic political success been scored by a version of the faith which lacks these traits, and is on the contrary endowed with their opposites? The paradox of the Iranian revolution is that whilst, on the one hand, Khomeini's movement benefited enormously from the distinctively Shi'ite characteristics in the process of revolutionary mobilization, nevertheless, in the process of attaining success and political power, Khomeini shifted Iranian Shi'ism firmly in the direction of a kind of 'Sunnification'. He took it very close to the puritan version of Sunni High Islam.[20]

Shi'ism is heavily centred on the reverence of sacred, divine personalities, and above all on its martyrs. Their martyrdom is kept vividly alive in folk memory by annual passion plays. Shi'ism has a certain resemblance not merely to Folk Islam but also to Christianity. The centrality of the martyrs means that Shi'ite scholars are not merely lawyer-theologians, but also experts on the biography of the crucial martyr.[21] This means that they are much better equipped to communicate with the masses in a state of political effervescence than are their Sunni counterparts. Martyrdom is rousing stuff, more so than pedantic points of theology and law. The fact that the original martyrdom was imposed by a formally Muslim ruler makes the invocation of precedent against a Muslim tyrant particularly effective. All this was used very effectively, during that building-up of mass hysteria which induced the revolutionaries to allow themselves to be mown down by the Shah's men in such numbers that eventually they broke the nerve of the opposition.

But though these personal martyrdom themes were heavily and decisively employed in the revolution itself, the Shi'ism eventually presented by Khomeini as the charter of the new regime was quite different. For one thing, petty saints were firmly told to mend their ways or face the consequences:

Khomeini shared the standard reformist views of the self-appointed folk providers of mediation. As for the unique, literally divine but hidden Imams, the ultimate founts of legitimacy, those terminators of the infinite regress of interpretation – they were, politically speaking, pensioned off. Khomeini did not deny that should the Hidden Imam return, he would rule, and that he alone would be the legitimate ruler. But he would take on government as an extra chore, somewhat grudgingly, and his political role would be quite distinct from his divinity. Above all, government would not be in the very least different from what it had been under the deputies of the Hidden Imam, the scholars.

The essence of government on his view was the implementation of divine law, neither more nor less. It should be implemented neither more nor less severely before or after the return of the Hidden Imam. It would be the same law and the same severity, neither diminished nor enhanced. It was the law which mattered, not he who implemented it.[22] So the centrality of law replaced that of the person.

Khomeini also moved Shi'ism in the direction of his rather distinctive republicanism: in effect, the republic of scholars. This was always implicit in the formal logic of Shi'ism, but political realities had obliged Persian Shi'ites in the past to accommodate themselves to a kind of caretaker monarchy. Tribes were required for a political revolution, and the tribal leader would become Shah. This need is no longer operative under modern conditions, and so the egalitarian, anti-mediationist streak in Islam can play itself out to the full. Scholars of the faith can rule without a tribal power base. In a semi-modern state, that base is no longer required.

To continue the argument: in Islam, we see a pre-industrial faith, a founded, doctrinal, world religion in the proper sense, which, at any rate for the time being, totally and effectively defies the secularization thesis. So far, there is no indication that it will succumb to secularization in the future either, though of course it is always dangerous to indulge in prophecy. The reasons which have made this achievement possible seem to be the following: all 'under-developed' countries tend to face a certain dilemma. (By 'under-developed' countries I mean any society affected by a deep economic-military inferiority, such as it can only remedy by reforming itself fundamentally. France was under-developed in the eighteenth century, and Germany at the beginning of the nineteenth.) The dilemma such countries face is: should we emulate those whom we wish to equal in power (thereby spurning our own tradition), or should we, on the contrary, affirm the values of our own tradition, even at the price of material weakness? This issue was most poignantly recorded in Russian literature of the nineteenth century in the form of the debate between Westernization and Populism/Slavophilism.

It is painful to spurn one's own tradition, but it is also painful to remain weak. Few under-developed countries have escaped this dilemma, and they have handled it in diverse ways. But what is interesting, and crucial for our argument, is that Islam is ideally placed to escape it.

The trauma of the Western impact (appearing in diverse Muslim countries at different points of time, stretching from the late eighteenth to the twentieth centuries) did not, amongst Muslim thinkers, provoke that intense polarization between Westernizers and Populists, *à la Russe*. Muslims seldom idealize their own folk tradition; they leave vicarious populism to Europeans imbued with the T. E. Lawrence syndrome. The situation provoked a quite different reaction. The urge to reform, ever present in Islam, acquired a new vigour and intensity. No doubt it also acquired some new themes and additional motivation: why has the West overtaken us, why is it such a menace to us?

But the dominant and persuasive answer recommended neither emulation of the West, nor idealization of some folk virtue and wisdom. It commended a *return* to, or a more rigorous observance of, *High* Islam. Admittedly this was linked to the historically perhaps questionable assumption that High Islam had once dominated and pervaded the whole of society, and also that it was identical with *early* Islam, with the teaching and practice of the Prophet and His Companions. This is questionable; but what is certainly true is that High Islam

19

constituted a perfectly genuine local tradition, and one long established, even if it has not succeeded in pervading the entire society, and whether or not it is really identical with the practice of the first generation(s) of Muslims.

So self-correction did not need to go outside the society, nor seek pristine virtue in its social depths: it could find it in its own perfectly genuine and real Higher Culture, which had indeed only been practised by a minority in the past, but which had been recognized (though not implemented) as a valid norm by the rest of society. Now, seemingly under the impact of a moral impulse and in response to preaching, but in fact as a result of profound and pervasive changes in social organization, it could at long last be practised by *all*. Self-reform in the light of modern requirements could be presented as a *return* to the genuinely local ideal, a moral home-coming, rather than a self-repudiation.

It is this vision which has now conquered the Muslim world. As an ideology of self-rectification, of purification, of recovery, it has a number of very considerable and striking advantages. It does not appeal to an *alien* model; it appeals to a model which has unquestionable, deep, genuine local roots. It may or may not really be identical with the real practice of the first generations of Muslims; but it *does* correspond to what so to speak normative, respected individuals and classes had preached and practised for a very long time. A man who turns to Reformist Islam does not, like a Westernizer in nineteenth-century Russia, thereby convey his contempt for his own ancestors and tradition. On the contrary, he re-affirms what he considers the best elements in the local culture, and which were genuinely present. And a man who turns to Reformist Islam is also close to 'the people', to what countless petty bourgeois actually practise, and to what many peasants aspire to practise, without at the same time committing himself to any implausible, far-fetched idealization of peasant or shepherd life as such. At the same time, whilst it is truly local, and genuinely resonates throughout the whole of society, this reformist ideal is also severely demanding, and unambiguously condemns and reprobates that folk culture which can, with some show of plausibility, be blamed for 'backwardness', and for the humiliation imposed by the West. High Islam had always opposed the ecstatic, undisciplined, personality-oriented variant of Islam. Now it could oppose it and be reinforced with some new arguments: it was *this* that had held us back! Not only have we so slid back from the shining example set us by the Prophet and the early Muslims, but in so doing we also made it easy for the infidel to humble us. The colonialists had exploited, or indeed encouraged and fomented, the worst streaks in our own culture. In this way the old impulse towards self-reformation and purification blends with reactive nationalism: it is indeed exceedingly hard to separate the two.

Weberian sociology leads us to expect a certain congruence between a modern economy and its associated beliefs and culture.[23] The modern mode of production is claimed, above all, to be 'rational'. It is orderly, sensitive to cost-effectiveness, thrifty rather than addicted to display, much given to the division of labour and the use of a free market. It requires those who operate it to be sensitive to the notion of obligation and the fulfilment of contract, to be work-oriented, disciplined, and not too addicted to economically irrelevant political and religious patronage networks, nor to dissipate too much of their energy in festivals or display. If this is indeed what a modern economy demands, and, above all, if this is what is required by the process of *construction* of a modern economy (and perhaps also of a modern polity), then Reformist Islam would seem to be custom-made for the needs of the hour. In fact, given the congruence between what Weberian sociology would lead one to expect, and what is offered by High and Reformist Islam, there is a bit of a puzzle concerning why Muslim economic performance is not rather more distinguished than it actually is. The economies of Muslim developing countries are not catastrophic, but they are not brilliant either, which is what the preceding argument might have led one to expect. Given the distorting effect of oil wealth, it is of course not easy to pass a definitive judgement.

But, whatever the state of the economy, there cannot be much doubt about the present situation in the ideological sphere. In the West, we have become habituated to a certain picture, according to which puritan zeal had accompanied the early stages of the emergence of a modern economy, but in which its culmination was eventually marked by a very widespread religious lukewarmness and secularization. The sober thrifty work-oriented spirit, which helps amass wealth, is then undermined by the seductions brought along by that which it has achieved. The virtue inculcated by puritanism leads to a prosperity which subverts that virtue itself, as John Wesley had noted with regret.

In the world of Islam, we encounter quite a different situation. Though long endowed with a commercial bourgeoisie and significant urbanization, this civilization failed to engender industrialism; but once industrialism and its various accompaniments had been thrust upon it, and it had experienced not only the resulting disturbance but also some of its benefits, it turned, not at all to secularization, but rather to a vehement affirmation of the puritan version of its own tradition. Perhaps this virtue has not yet been rewarded by a really generalized affluence, but there is little to indicate that a widespread affluence would erode religious commitment. Even the unearned oil-fall wealth has not had this effect.

Things may yet change in the future. But on the evidence available so far, the world of Islam demonstrates that it is possible to run a modern, or at any rate modernizing, economy, reasonably permeated by the appropriate technological, educational, organization principles, *and* combine it with a strong, pervasive, powerfully internalized Muslim conviction and identification. A puritan and scripturalist world religion does not seem necessarily doomed to erosion by modern conditions. It may on the contrary be favoured by them.

POSTMODERNISM AND RELATIVISM

Postmodernism is a contemporary movement. It is strong and fashionable. Over and above this, it is not altogether clear what the devil it is. In fact, clarity is not conspicuous amongst its marked attributes. It not only generally fails to practise it, but also on occasion actually repudiates it. But anyway, there appear to be no 39 postmodernist Articles of faith, no postmodernist Manifesto, which one could consult so as to assure oneself that one has identified its ideas properly.

The influence of the movement can be discerned in anthropology,[24] literary studies, philosophy. It tends to bring these fields far closer to each other than they had been previously. The notions that everything is a 'text', that the basic material of texts, societies and almost anything is meaning, that meanings are there to be decoded or 'deconstructed', that the notion of objective reality is suspect – all this seems to be part of the atmosphere, or mist, in which postmodernism flourishes, or which postmodernism helps to spread.

I am not entirely clear about the attitude of the movement to the human subject: sometimes there seems to be an enormous preoccupation with him, so that a social anthropological study degenerates from having been a study of a society into a study of the reaction of the anthropologist to his own reactions to his observations of the society, assuming that he had ever got as far as to have made any. The pursuit of generalization, in the image of science, is excoriated as 'positivism', so 'theory' tends to become a set of pessimistic and obscure musings on the Inaccessibility of the Other and its Meanings. At other times, the gimmick seems to be to exile the author from the text and to proceed to decode, or deconstruct, or de-something, the meanings which spoke through the author, had he but known it.

The movement and its ideas are, I fear, a little too ethereal and volatile to be captured and seized with precision: perhaps the acute awareness of the movement that all meanings are to be deconstructed in a way which also brings in their opposites, and highlights the contradictions contained in them, or something like that, actually precludes a crisp and unambiguous formulation of the position. In any case, if this is to be done, it had better be done by someone else: I do not feel too much at home at these heights or in these depths. This is *nur für Schwindelfreie*, of whose number I am not.

But there is a certain theme within this cluster of ideas which does profoundly concern the present argument, and that is *relativism*. Postmodernism would seem to be rather clearly in favour of relativism, in as far as it is capable of clarity, and hostile to the idea of unique, exclusive, objective, external or transcendent truth. Truth is elusive, polymorphous, inward, subjective . . . and perhaps a few further things as well. Straightforward it is not. My real concern is with *relativism*: the postmodernist movement, which is an ephemeral cultural fashion, is of interest as a living and contemporary specimen of relativism, which as such is of some importance and will remain with us for a long time.

Wittgenstein once said (in the course of formulating his initial, subsequently repudiated, philosophy) that the world is not the totality of things, but of facts. In the current intellectual atmosphere, one senses a feeling that the world is not the totality of things, but of meanings. Everything is meaning, and meaning is everything, and hermeneutics is its prophet. Whatever is, is made by the meaning conferred on it. It is the meaning with which it is endowed which has singled it out from the primal flow of uncategorized existence, and thereby turned it into an identifiable object. (But the meaning which confers existence also assigns status, and so is a tool of domination.) It is perhaps this fusion of subjectivity and hermeneutics with a self-righteous promise – and monopoly? – of liberation which endows this outlook with its distinctive character. The *subject* had once been a kind of refuge, a redoubt: even if we could not be sure of the outside world, we could at least be certain of our own feelings, thoughts and sensations. But no: if these are engendered by *meanings* imposed on inchoate unidentifiable raw material, and meanings come in self-contradictory cultural packages, then no such certainty and resting point is to be found inside ourselves! The Cartesian redoubt has been taken! We must distrust our subjectivity as much as our erstwhile claims to know the Other. Modernists in literature had turned to the subject, to the privacy of the stream of consciousness: postmodernists unmask the mechanisms and functions of subjectivity, locate the rules of objectivity within it, and destabilize everything.

So the movement locates itself all at once both in the context of world politics and in the context of the history of world thought. The two *prises de position* are related to each other.

In the history of the social sciences, the movement considers itself part and parcel of a switch from what it likes to call 'positivism' to hermeneutics. As Fardon puts it:

> The precise date of a current revolution is contentious, but witnesses from the 1970s onwards began to detect . . . that the grounds of knowledge were moving. The earth tremblings . . . came to be named postmodernism . . . and . . . recognised as more general doubts about . . . scientific . . . models of human behaviour. . . . Preoccupation with text, and with a vocabulary of narrativity, empletment, ultra-commentary . . . is symptomatic.[25]

Positivism would appear to mean a belief in the existence and availability of objective facts, and above all in the possibility of explaining the said facts by means of an objective and testable theory, not itself essentially linked to any one culture, observer or mood. What seems to be the very devil is the supposition that a theory could be articulated, understood, assessed, without any reference to its author and his social identity. First the specification, and then the so to speak diminution, of the author-inquirer is the speciality of this outlook.

Positivism in this sense is challenged all along this line: facts are inseparable from the observer who claims to discern them, and the culture which supplied the categories in terms of which they are described. This being so, he had better tell us about himself. He had better confess his culture. Real, self or culture-independent facts in any case being neither available nor accessible, there is not much else he can tell us. Even what he tells us about himself is suspect and tortuous. So he does tell us about himself with relish, and seldom gets much further; and, given the premises of the movement, it would be quite wrong of him if he did get much further. It would show that he failed to learn the deep doubts which are the movement's speciality.

There are, strictly speaking, two distinct points, though they tend to interact and feed into each other. There is the point that characterization of human conduct is meaning-pervaded, and that in the study of members of one culture by those of another, *two* sets of meanings, and the problem of their mutual intelligibility and translatability, are involved. We are not dealing with hard unambiguous facts, whose conceptual packaging is translucent and uncontentious. (Are we ever?) Secondly, there is the fact that the observer is a being of flesh and blood, with expectations, interests, prejudices, blind spots, and this raises a problem even if he happened to be of the same culture as those whom he is studying, drawing on pretty much the same set of concepts. In practice, these two considerations tend to reinforce each other in making for a double, not really separated, shift from thing to meaning, and from object to subject, to a kind of narcissism-hermeneuticism.

In world history, the period since the Second World War has been, amongst other things, the period of decolonization, the termination of that overt European domination of the world which had begun with the great voyages of discovery, and which reached its peak in the early twentieth century. Part of the system of ideas under consideration seems to be the claim that the two processes are linked: colonialism went with positivism, decolonization with hermeneutics, and it eventually culminates in postmodernism. Positivism is a form of imperialism, or perhaps the other way round, or both. Lucidly presented and (putatively) independent facts were the tool and expression of colonial domination; by contrast, subjectivism signifies intercultural equality and respect. The world as it truly is (if indeed it may ever truly be said to be anything) is made up of tremulous subjectivities; objective facts and generalizations are the expressions and tools of domination!

In a way, the whole confrontation might be seen as a kind of replay of the battle between classicism and romanticism, the former associated with the domination of Europe by a French court and its manners and standards, and the latter with the eventual reaction by other nations, affirming the values of their own folk cultures.[26] As far as I know, this parallel has not been drawn before. In our time, moreover, it was not only the ex-colonial nations who attained liberation; it was also the period of the feminist movement, and of various other self-affirmation movements by minority or oppressed groups. Women constitute one such group, and a specially vocal one, and so gender as well as meaning become prominent. But the romantics wrote poetry; the postmodernists also indulge their subjectivism, but their repudiation of formal discipline, their expression of deep inner turbulence, is performed in aca-demese prose, intended for publication in learned journals, a means of securing promotion by impressing the appropriate committees. *Sturm und Drang und Tenure* might well be their slogan.

So one pervasive and oft-recurring theme within the move-ment insists on the connection between the two sets of events, between political liberation and cognitive subjectivity. Clarity and the insistence on – or, rather, the imposition of – an allegedly unique and objective reality is simply a tool, or per-haps, in some versions, the preferred tool, of domination. The objectivism aspired to or invoked by traditional, pre-modern social science was covertly a means of imposing a vision on men, which constrained those dominated to accept their sub-jection. It is not entirely clear whether the violation consisted of imposing a certain *particular* vision, confirming the estab-lished order, on its victims, or whether the main sin was the imposition of the very ideal of objectivity. Is the aspiration to objectivity as such the cardinal sin?

There is a corresponding ambiguity concerning the con-trasted, virtuous, liberating vision. Does it consist of a multi-plicity of theories, all separate but equal, or in the abstention from theory altogether, and the restriction of social knowledge simply to the acquisition, perhaps the expounding, of ethno-graphic texts? It would seem that the movement vacillates between a theoretical free-for-all and a non-theoretical or anti-theoretical collection of unique, idiosyncratic meanings. On occasion, what seems to be envisaged is a collage of statements drawn from the people investigated and from the investigators, commenting on their own cognitive anguish.

It all seems to lead to something called 'dialogic' and

'heteroglossic' styles of presentation, which avoids presenting unique facts, and replaces them by *multiple* voices. James Clifford, one of the editors of the text I am using as a specimen of this style,[27] is also quoted within the volume itself, as follows:

> Dialogic and constructivist paradigms tend to disperse or share out ethnographic authority. . . . Paradigms of experience and interpretation are yielding to paradigms of discourse, or dialogue and polyphony.

The essay itself, by P. Rabinow, goes on to ask 'What is dialogic?',[28] only to conclude on the next page that 'the genre's defining characteristics remain unclear'. Quite so, but given that the dialogic is meant to be a great step forward, this is rather surprising. The definition which would have had it consist of representing dialogues is at first offered, with the suggestion that it is at least an approximation, but then abandoned as too simple.

But there is the further revelation, 'heteroglossia'. Clifford is quoted again:[29]

> Ethnography is invaded by heteroglossia . . . indigenous statements make sense on terms different from those of the arranging ethnographer. . . . This suggests an alternate [sic] textual strategy, a utopia of plural authorship that accords to collaborators, not merely the status of independent enunciators, but of writers.

It all seems to amount to a kind of collage – a few pages later we are indeed referred to pastiche and hotchpotch – with a vacillation between the hope that this multiplicity of voices somehow excludes the bias of the external researcher, and a pleasurable return to a guilty recognition that the subject, the author, is still there. What these authors seem to be after is to eliminate all clarity, all objectivity, but in the end not to deprive themselves of the pleasure of still feeling guilty about a residue of observer's intrusion. In the end, they are still there, however hard they strove to escape through 'dialogue', 'heteroglossia', or whatever. All those stylistic innovations are meant to bring the informant right into the book, undistorted by interpretation: but this is followed by the agreeably sinful realization that, after all, the author(s) had brought him there, in a context which also constitutes interpretation. There is no escape and the authors wouldn't really wish to escape their sin. The guilt seems to be far too pleasurable.

It is almost impossible to give a coherent definition or account of postmodernism. The reader is advised to look at two paragraphs by Rabinow in the work we have used[30] which in fact begin with the question – 'What is post-modernism?' All one can say is that it is a kind of hysteria of subjectivity which goes beyond 'Joyce, Hemingway, Woolf, et al.', who evidently did not go far enough: their 'conceit of an interiorized and distinctive subjectivity . . . both drew from and stood at a distance from normal speech and identity'. Far too orderly, it would seem. Going further, it seems one reaches a point when the tension between normality and modernity cracks (*sic*), abandoning 'the assumption . . . of relatively stable identity and linguistic norms'.

What it all means is less than clear – the metaphysical-lit. crit. jargon takes care of that – but the theory, such as it is, feeds back on its own style and underwrites its chaos and obscurity: the insight itself calls for abandonment of 'linguistic norms', and is articulated in accordance with its own discoveries. What it means in literature does not concern me; in anthropology, it means in effect the abandonment of any serious attempt to give a reasonably precise, documented and testable account of anything. It is also unclear why, given that universities already employ people to explain why knowledge is impossible (in philosophy departments), anthropology departments should reduplicate this task, in somewhat amateurish fashion.

In the end, the operational meaning of postmodernism in anthropology seems to be something like this: a refusal (in practice, rather selective) to countenance any objective facts, any independent social structures, and their replacement by a pursuit of 'meanings', both those of the objects of inquiry and of the inquirer. There is thus a double stress on subjectivity: the world-creation by the person studied, and the text-creation by the investigator. 'Meaning' is less a tool of analysis than a conceptual intoxicant, an instrument of self-titillation. The investigator demonstrates both his initiation into the mysteries of hermeneutics, and the difficulty of the enterprise, by complex and convoluted prose, peppered with allusions to a high proportion of the authors of the World's 100 Great Books, and also to the latest fashionable scribes of the Left Bank. The names used in the references generally read as if they had been copied from the Paris Metro map, minor stops on the route to the Porte d'Orléans. The jerky fragmentariness also practised is one of the ways of conveying that postmodernism is well beyond the relatively tidy stream-of-consciousness subjectivism, practised as part of the mere old-fashioned modernisms of a Joyce or Proust or Woolf.

The link between political and hermeneutic egalitarianism is heavily stressed, and indeed seems self-evident to the participants in the movement. In the days of imperial and/or patriarchal power, the rulers (colonialists or partriarchs or indeed colonialist patriarchs) used their power to impose their vision on their victims; or, rather, used their vision and its authority to attain their power or to make it secure, and impose the illusion of its legitimacy on their victims. Presumably they did not merely want slaves, but slaves who internalized their subjection *in the name of objectivity*. One could sum it all up by saying that the whole idea of objectivity and clarity is simply a cunning trick of dominators. Descartes had simply prepared the ground for Kipling. Descartes, *ergo* Kipling. No Kipling, so no Descartes. Liberty makes its reappearance in the form of a logically permissive and pluralist obscurity. The negation of Kipling also requires the repudiation of Descartes. In fact Descartes, who initiated the determined pursuit of an objective truth untainted by cultural blinkers, a Reason untainted by 'custom and example' (his own term for culture), had forged the tools and weapons which were required for a colonialist-patriarchal domination of the earth. Descartes had claimed to use the *cogito* as a premiss so as to escape cultural blinkers. Over three centuries it returns with a vengeance as a device for locating and affirming them, as the only reality.

This vision has a number of possible intellectual ancestors. One of them, strangely enough, is Marxism. This is of course somewhat paradoxical, given that Marxism claims to be a 'materialism', and to be committed to a vision of social life which ascribes primacy to material forces of production, and that it consequently treats systems of meaning as merely secondary and derivative. It proudly claimed to be 'scientific', and indeed to constitute the final culmination of the application of science to society and to moral issues. It certainly claimed to be in possession of *objective* truth. This may indeed have been the original Marxist vision, born as it was from a revulsion against a Hegelian idealism which, in its own time, also had, in its own distinctive and now rather antiquated terminology, interpreted the world as an externalization of meanings. Marxism had begun by inventing and repudiating all this, and presenting meanings as the echo of real, objective forces.

But that was a long time ago, in a dawn in which it was bliss to be alive, and much water has passed under the bridge since. The absolutist-exclusive quality of the Marxist revelation, and the manner in which it was presented and perpetuated, meant that Marxists always found it difficult to credit those who did not accept their vision with good faith. Moreover, their own theory required them to *explain* those dissidents sociologically. Error was not random, but socially functional: the specification of its function not merely identified and unmasked the heretic, but also illuminated the social scene. The enemy's erroneous views highlighted his position, the social ills he was concerned to defend, and the means available to him for this nefarious purpose. The denunciation and unmasking was an education as well as a pleasure.

The Marxist rapidly acquired a strong taste for, and skill at, such reductive explanation, and the explaining-away of critical opinion in terms of the class experience and interest of the critic became a well-established literary style, with its canons, its classics, its habitual procedures. With the passage of time, and especially after the establishment of the Soviet Union, the amount of hostile criticism which needed to be explained away grew at an ever increasing pace, and the proportion of Marxism consisting of denunciatory explanations of the *denials* of Marxism augmented correspondingly. Marxism became almost a kind of special subject, whose province was the collective cultural delusions, the world-constructions, of *others*.

This differed from the movement which concerned us now in two respects: the attitude to the world-creations investigated was somewhat negative rather than deferential, and there still remained a residual unique and objective truth which was to be affirmed – though the amount of attention this residue received was rapidly diminishing. But the strange result of all this was that Marxism tended to approximate, not a historical materialism, but rather a historical subjectivism, its practitioners becoming enormously adept at invoking the philosophical ploys which deny objectivity. Sometimes this habit simply took over completely.

This entire tendency was developed further by an influential movement which was no longer linked to international Communism and thus was free from any obligation to defend the record of applied Marxism – the philosophical movement known as the Frankfurt School, and its so-called 'Critical Theory'. This itself was fairly typical of the liberation of international left-wing intelligentsia from Communist Party authority and discipline, which followed Khrushchev's revelations to the XXth Congress of the CPSU(B). It provided much of the ideology for student protest of the 1960s, which was critical of *both* the then dominant world camps.

The Frankfurt School resembled the party-bound Marxists in being much given to explaining-away of the views of its opponents; but there was an interesting difference. The old-fashioned Marxists did not oppose the very notion of objectivity, as such, they merely maintained that their opponents had failed to be *genuinely* objective, and merely pretended to observe the norms of scientific objectivity, whilst in reality serving, and being misled by, their own class interests. But real science still remained, and was contrasted with class-interest-inspired false consciousness. There was, however, in the attitude of the old-fashioned, so to speak square, Marxists, a foretaste of what was to come, in as far as they would stress that the observance of merely 'formal' procedural scientific propriety was not sufficient, and was indeed a camouflage: *real* objectivity required, above all, a sound class and political position. It was fairly easy to slide from this to the view that a sound position was sufficient on its own, and, finally, the view that there are no 'sound', objective positions at all. The real delusion was the belief in the possibility of objective, unique truth. Thought lives on meanings, meanings are culture-bound. *Ergo*, life is subjectivity.

So the difference was that the old Marxists respected objectivity as such, and merely charged their opponents with failing to practise it properly, and with violating it whilst pretending to serve it. What was distinctive about the Frankfurters was a tendency to decry the cult of objective fact as such, and not merely its alleged misapplications. An excessively fastidious, methodologically punctilious preoccupation with *what is*, was, under the guise of disinterested inquiry, an attempt to legitimate *that which was*, by somehow insinuating that nothing else could be.[31] A real, enlightened, *critical* thinker (*à la* Frankfurt) did not waste too much time, or probably did not waste any time at all, on finding out precisely what *was*; he went straight to the hidden substance under the surface, the deep features which explained just why that which *was*, was, and also to the equally deep illumination concerning what *should be*. Unenslaved to the positivist cult of what *was*, the investigation of which was but a camouflaged ratification of the status quo, a genuinely critical free spirit found himself in a good position to determine just what it was that should be, in dialectical opposition to that which merely *was*. Those were the days when a 'positivist' was a man invoking facts against Marxism; nowadays, he is anyone who makes use of facts at all, or allows their existence, whatever his aim.

Such, in substance, was the creed of the student rebels of the 1960s and in particular of 1968, the theme of *One-Dimensional Man*[32] as formulated for them by Marcuse, Adorno, and others. The Frankfurt School possessed moderately clear and interesting, though not unduly original, ideas concerning just why one should not be too enslaved to *what is*.[33] They held that the postwar affluence and 'End of Ideology' mood was but an attempt to absolutize *what was*, and to deny that anything else could be.

What they did not possess – or if they did possess it, they kept it marvellously secret – was any even remotely precise or plausible or concrete method for determining either that deep truth which lay beneath the merely superficial facts beloved by the despised 'positivists', or for determining just which alternative social possibility was to be held up to current reality as a preferable, and realistic, ideal. After all, there is a countless number of possible deep explanations of the surface (and the number of possible explanations presumably becomes even greater if, imbued with contempt for the surface facts, you do not even know just what those facts are); and, similarly, there is a countless number of possible contrasts to or negations of the present situation, all of which some of us might prefer to the current reality. How is one to choose the right one? Answer came there none. In practice, the Frankfurters and their followers, freed by their elevated depth (Karl Popper's apt phrase) from any tedious superficial positivist fact-grubbing, gave themselves licence to disclose their own private revelations or intuitions concerning both the deep and the ideal. The Alternative was conjured up by hocus-pocus, sleight of hand and verbiage. But they did at least pretend that they had a method for so doing, and so they paid lip-service to the ideal of objectivity and method, even if they sinned against it in practice. No 'critical method' really existed, but the pretence that it did exist was a compliment which subjectivism payed to objectivity.

The postmodernists continue the trajectory whose earlier points had been occupied by the old Marxists and the Frankfurters, though this is not ancestry they themselves stress unduly.[34] The Frankfurters had picked on, not so much specific distortion of real objectivity, but rather the cult of objectivity as such: this was the source of distortion, and it was their task to rectify it. No cult of superficial facts please! But they still retained the notion of an alternative sound position, at least in principle, as an ideal – one alleged to be genuinely objective, which was to be contrasted with the error they so enthusiastically diagnosed and described – however nebulous, unspecified and inherently arbitrary and wilfully manipulable that alternative salvation was. They recognized it in principle, and, moreover, they believed themselves to be in possession of it.

The postmodernists have gone one step further. Like the Frankfurters they repudiate the cult and pursuit of extraneous facts, which are mistakenly held to provide the path to perception of social reality, but they no longer replace it by an (obscurely specified) alternative path, but by the affirmation that no such path is either possible or necessary or desirable. It isn't *superficial* objectivity which is repudiated, but objectivity as such. The oppressive enemies are credited not with peddling a wrong and spurious objectivity (as opposed to a good and genuine one), but for being in error, in political and cognitive sin, by seeking objectivity at all. The article of R. Fardon's quoted above suggests that they see as their immediate predecessor, whom they are transcending, the *structuraliste* movement, which was also preoccupied with culture, but thought it could de-compose a culture into its binary constituents, on the lines of a method which had, it seems, worked well enough in the simpler world of phonetics.

Objective truth is to be replaced by hermeneutic truth. Hermeneutic truth respects the subjectivity both of the object of the inquiry and of the inquirer, and even of the reader or listener. In fact the practitioners of the method are so deeply, so longingly, imbued both by the difficulty and the undesirability of transcending the meanings – of their objects, of themselves, of their readers, of anyone – that in the end one tends to be given poems and homilies on the locked circles of meaning in which everyone is imprisoned, excruciatingly *and* pleasurably.

Bertrand Russell once spoke of the 'egocentric predicament', the problem in the theory of knowledge arising from the fact that the individual subject is confined to the closed circle of his own current sensations, and has no way of reaching knowledge beyond them. Our actual data give us neither a past nor a future, neither permanent objects nor law-governed order, nor other people; they give us themselves only, and a strict empiricism, forswearing any leap to the unobserved, does not allow us to proceed any further. The postmodernists have discovered – or, at any rate, celebrated and exploited – another and rather different version of the egocentric predicament, in which the individual is imprisoned in the circle, no longer of his immediate sensations, but of his meanings. The empiricist redoubt of certainty in the self and its immediate awareness is thereby captured and destroyed – for even these inner perceptions are meaning-saturated, and those meanings in turn are culture-bound, contradictory, and deserving of 'deconstruction'. So the postmodernist will try to communicate the anguish of his field experience, in which he and his subjects tried to break out of their respective islands and reach out to each other. Of course, they must fail! Not to fail, to succeed, to come back with a clear, neat, crisp account of what the natives actually mean, would be a most dreadful disgrace and betrayal for our postmodernist. That would constitute the final treason and *real* failure. It would show him up as a superficial positivist, at the service of colonialism and the inequality of cultures, claiming to pin down the Other in terms of his *own* meanings, thereby suborning and lowering the Other, and revealing himself as a man insensitive to the infinite idiosyncrasy of all meanings, and the equally infinite difficulty of communicating them or conveying them across that dreadful chasm separating one realm of significance from another.

There are of course at least two such chasms, one between the postmodernist investigator and the informant, and the other between the writer and his audience. Facing each of these chasms, our postmodernist will prove his trans-positivist sophistication and sensitivity by being overwhelmed by both of them, and displaying his real depth, his awareness of the hermeneutic problem, by demonstratively failing to cross either, dissolving into chaos, impenetrable prose, and speaking in tongues. Strictly speaking, the rest should (logically) be silence. But postmodernists do publish, sometimes quite a lot, and have evidently not quite brought themselves to embrace fully this logical corollary of their depth. But perhaps there are some really good postmodernists who in fact do not publish at all? *Ex hypothesi*, a really good one would be silent. Perhaps some real genius of postmodernism will one day persuade us to admire his uniquely deep silence, rather like the avant-garde painter who secures admiration for a canvas which he simply covers with uniform black paint.

So the path leads from Marxist elimination of opponents for alleged pseudo-objectivity, to Frankfurt castigation of superficial positivism equated with the amassing of surface facts, to postmodernist repudiation of the very aspiration to objectivity, and its replacement by hermeneutics: this is the one line of logical development which strikes me, whether or not it really corresponds to the participants' own view of their intellectual ancestry, or to the actual historical links. That remains to be explored and documented.

There is also an alternative and also rather interesting path, leading from the alleged overcoming of the theory of knowledge, of 'epistemology', an overcoming which is acclaimed as the great achievement of twentieth-century philosophy. It is associated with names such as Wittgenstein, Heidegger, Rorty, and others.[35] In as far as epistemology is an inquiry into the difficulties facing the mind in its pursuit of knowledge of external reality, one might have expected that a movement so acutely imbued with a sense of these difficulties, indeed one which turns them into a kind of self-titillating house speciality, would treat epistemology as a welcome ally. But this is not always so.

The point is that the great epistemological tradition in Western philosophy (now claimed to be overcome), stretching from Descartes to Hume and Kant and beyond, formulated the problem of knowledge, not in terms of a kind of egalitarian hermeneuticism, or of hermeneutic egalitarianism, but, rather, in terms of a discriminating cognitive élitism. It did indeed hold all men and minds, but *not* all cultures and systems of meaning, to be equal. All minds were endowed with the potential of attaining a unique objective truth, but only on condition of employing the correct method and forswearing the seduction of cultural indoctrination. Culture (which Descartes named

37

'custom and example') was, in the Cartesian programme, *the* source of error. That is of course an abomination to those imbued with the postmodernist spirit. What Descartes and his successors said, in effect, was that there are an awful lot of meanings and opinions about, that they cannot all be right, and that we'd better find, and justify, a yardstick which will sort out the sheep from the goats. For Descartes, the yardstick involved the exclusive use of *clear and distinct* meanings, so clear and distinct as to impose their authority on all minds sober and determined enough to heed them, irrespective of their culture. The path to truth lay through voluntary cultural exile. The terms of reference of the central, classical theory of knowledge included the assumption that there *was* a right and wrong way of going about the acquisition of knowledge: the problem was to find the difference, and, when it was located, to justify it. The contemporary idea is that there is no difference, that to set up ranking between kinds of knowledge is morally and politically wicked, rather like setting up one skin colour above another (with more than a hint that perhaps the two discriminations were linked to each other).

The manner in which the new turn in philosophy, the alleged overcoming of the old unique-truth-seeking epistemology, relates to the postmodernist movement is offered, with insight and not without humour, by a member of the movement, Paul Rabinow. Discussing the work of one of the thinkers who has contributed to the formulation and the elaboration of this new vision, Richard Rorty, Rabinow says, in the volume edited by Clifford and Marcus which comes close to being a kind of manifesto of the movement, and which we have been using:[36]

These thinkers did not seek to construct alternate [*sic*] or better theories of the mind or knowledge. Their aim was not to improve epistemology but to play a different game. Rorty calls this game hermeneutics. By this, he simply means knowledge without foundation; a knowledge that essentially amounts to edifying conversation. Rorty has so far told us very little about the content of this conversation, perhaps because there is very little to tell.

Rabinow evidently approves Rorty's basic position, but as the touch of irony which he allows himself already conveys, he does not think Rorty goes nearly far enough. Rorty would, at any rate according to Rabinow, merely proceed from the old theory of knowledge, which had acted as a severe end-of-term examiner, failing many, passing few, and awarding *suma cum laude* to a very few, to a more tolerant, easy-going conversationalist, happy to chat with all and sundry and to damn none. Rabinow believes Rorty's insights to be complemented and developed by Foucault, and in the light of these improvements he proceeds to sketch out a programme for a new anthropology.[37]

> Epistemology must be seen as a historical event . . . one amongst many others, articulated in . . . seventeenth century Europe. . . . We do not need . . . a new epistemology. . . . We should be attentive to our historical practice of projecting our cultural practice onto the other. . . . We need to anthropologize the West: show how exotic its constitution of reality has been . . . a basic move against either economic or philosophic hegemony is to diversify centres of resistance: avoid the error of reverse essentializing: Occidentalism is not a remedy for Orientalism.

The last remark is of course an allusion to the charge that Western scholars have created an image of the East which is all at once a travesty, an imposition, and a means of subjugation and of domination. It won't do, says Rabinow, to do the same for the West: to do so would be to make *one* West, and plural relativism must apply within the West, or to hermeneutics of it, as much as it applies between it and the Orient(s) . . .

What the passage, however, does make clear is the link between the repudiation of the theory of knowledge and the new relativism. Epistemology had passed judgement on diverse kinds of knowledge, and that will never do.

RELATIVISMUS ÜBER ALLES

Is there such a thing as going *too far* in this direction? Rabinow in the work under discussion goes on to describe just how far this style can go, again not without perception and humour, though I am not quite clear whether he describes it with approval or reprobation (perhaps it doesn't matter). We have already quoted passages from the volumes concerning the direction in which ethnographic style is to go. Rabinow comments on the work of James Clifford (one of the editors of the volume in which the essay itself appears) noting first of all that there is an important difference between the work of James Clifford and that of Clifford Geertz, of which it might at first sight be held to be a continuation: Geertz, or all of his hermeneutic or interpretive turn, 'is still directing his efforts to reinvent anthropological science'.

But Clifford has gone beyond all that. Clifford is no longer interested in 'the Other' (i.e. the ethnographic object, other societies, cultures): the 'Other' for Clifford is the anthropological representation of the Other. Rabinow deconstructs Clifford's deconstruction of anthropologists' deconstruction of . . . Where will it all end? Clifford is not interested in the Navajo or Nuer or the Trobrianders, he is interested in what anthropologists say about them . . . How about someone only being interested in what Clifford says about what others say . . . ?

You may think that this was anticipation, with incredulity, hinting at a kind of *reductio ad absurdum* . . . Not a bit of it. It has already happened. Later on, Rabinow both reports and reformulates, and I think endorses, this further step in the regress. Apparently, even the ultimate postmodernist does not allow sufficiently for his/her subjectivity. In his/her very awareness of relativity, not merely between culture (old hat), people (likewise), but between successive moments or moods, lies his/her awareness:[38]

40

The post-modernist is blind to her own situation and situ-atedness because, qua post-modernist, she is so committed to a doctrine of partiality and flux for which even such things as one's own situation are so unstable, so without identity, that they cannot serve as objects of sustained reflection.

So don't think that, by refusing to absolutize even your fleeting mood, and dissolving into flux, you escape being decon-structed, unmasked, and being sent free-falling through the void. There is no escape. Relativizing critics will pursue you even into this lair, if so solid-sounding a metaphor may be allowed. And of course the pursuer will be pursued too, and so on forever. It really would be much better to have done with it all, and say that the rest is silence.

Within the whole tradition, it is incidentally possible to dis-cern two distinct arguments which are intertwined, but aren't really compatible. One of them is that the pursuit of objectivity is really spurious, and a form of domination: the observer insulates the objects and sits in judgement on it. (The style has a striking parallelism with Luigi Pirandello's device of suspending the customary separation between author, actor, character and audience.) But there is *also* the argument that the world has become more complex, and that the separation of roles is *no longer* possible (but was once practicable). It is indeed true that the world has become more tangled and unstable; but this, to my mind, shows only that objectivity is harder, not that it is inherently misguided and must be replaced by stylistic chaos and pastiche. If we note that the world has changed, we would seem to be in possession of some objective information about it after all.

The regress into subjectivity and navel-gazing, whatever its rationale, is also described in fine academic prose:[39]

The metareflections on the crisis of representations . . . indicate a shift away . . . to . . . concern with . . . metatra-ditions of metarepresentations . . .

There is no end to this metatwaddle.

41

And yet there is a hint of an underlying more or less coherent idea in all this: starting from the point which helped inspire epistemology, namely that there are tools used in knowledge, and that these deserve and require examination (whilst at the same time repudiating the epistemological aspiration to find out who is right and who is wrong), there is an attempt to link this to the indisputable fact that in this world there is a great deal of inequality of power (and other kinds of inequality, for that matter). Could there be a link between the way the tools of knowledge *make* the worlds which they claim to *find*, and those inequalities? A good question.

Unfortunately, members of this movement jump to conclusions a little too fast, with a tendency to answer the question by a facile Yes (to qualify the answer is to confess oneself a reactionary) and then, in an ambivalent attempt to find a way out of the relativist impasse, become ever more enmeshed in a regress in which nothing is allowed to stand, or everything stands and falls equally. They rather like this impasse, it constitutes their speciality, their distinction, their superiority over the poor benighted objectivists. Was it Tom Lehrer who commented in one of his splendid monologues on the kind of young American woman who talks endlessly about how impossible she finds it to *communicate* (which, significantly, has become an intransitive verb)?

The political connections of the ideas of the movement, as perceived by its members themselves, are well expressed in a contribution to the volume by one of its editors, George E. Marcus. In his essay 'Ethnography in the modern world system', we read:[40]

This move toward the ethnographic in American academic political economy . . . is related to a widely perceived decline of the post-World War II international order in which America held a hegemonic position. . . . A sense of profound transition in the foundations of domestic and international reality, as seen from the American perspective, has in turn been reflected intellectually in a widespread retreat from theoretically centralized and organized fields of knowledge. Goals of organizing scholarly practice in such diverse fields as history, the social sciences, literature, art and architecture have given way to fragmentation and . . . experimentation that aim to explore . . . and represent diversity. . . . Among the vehicles of experimentation, precocious in relation to this trend, is ethnography in anthropology.

That, in a way, says it all. To put it more simply: just after the War, the Americans dominated the world, and, in their thought, at least strove for order ('theoretically centralized and organized fields of knowledge'). Talcott Parsons and his group thought of themselves as the up-to-date Royal Society of the social sciences, close to revealing the ultimate secrets of the social system and on the verge of splitting the sociological atom (as Parsons once put it in conversation), and who would also advise America, at the moment it assumed the White Man's Burden, on how it should think about societies other than itself and the Navajo. With the loss of hegemony came the chaos, described as fragmentation and experimentation with a preference for detail, which is also meant to be (though this passage does not quite say so in so many words) an expiation of the erstwhile hegemony.

The authors of this volume conceive themselves as building on the 'interpretive' anthropology of Clifford Geertz, but going well beyond it. As we have seen, Rabinow observes with a touch of condescension that Geertz was still trying to do anthropology proper, albeit with the help of the new interpretive twist, whilst James Clifford was only studying anthropologists. But Geertz certainly set a precedent for this characteristically 'postmodernist' linking of domination and the pursuit of clarity and objectivity. But where Marcus links objectivist social science to American domination, Geertz devoted an important part of a book to the linking of classical Malinowskian anthropology, the British school, to British domination and imperial arrogance. Speaking of the British style of anthropology (in both senses of 'style'), he says, singling out Edward Evans-Pritchard in particular,[41] it seems to me a 'theatre of language' of enormous power – in ethnography, the most powerful yet constructed . . . the so-called 'British' school of social anthropology . . . is held together far more by this manner of going about things in prose than it is by any sort of consensual theory.

This bringing of Africans into a world conceived in deeply English terms, and confirming thereby the domination of those terms, must, however, not be misunderstood. [Nevertheless] . . . their differences from us . . . do not, finally, count for much.

Geertz contrasts this effortless domination and clarity of Evans-Pritchard with what has followed:[42]

The confidence that self-closing discourse gave . . . to Evans-Pritchard seems to many anthropologists less and less available. Not only are they confronted by societies half modern half traditional; by fieldwork conditions of staggering ethical complexity; by a host of wildly contrasting approaches to description and analysis; and by subjects who can speak and do speak for themselves. They are also harassed by grave inner uncertainties, amounting almost to a sort of epistemological hypochondria, concerning how one can know how anything one says about other forms of life is as a matter of fact so.

At the time Geertz wrote this, the hypochondria was, as they say in Yorkshire, no'but in its infancy. Since then, it has grown into a fine strapping lad. We have seen that the mild dose of it contracted by Geertz is surpassed by far by his defiant intellectual progeny, who now disavow him as not nearly sceptical, Hamlet-like, self-bound, postmodernist enough. Whatever Geertz's achievements in anthropology, his pro-relativism endorses and underwrites the excess of those who would go 'beyond him' along the path he has indicated. The first hypochondria was linked only to the repudiation of overt colonialism; the second stage, by contrast, is linked to the demise of

American hegemony, and the delight this gives to some members of the American academic profession.

Of course, one could dismiss the whole trend, saying something like this. This posturing has gone far enough. Geertz has encouraged a whole generation of anthropologists to parade their real or invented inner qualms and paralysis, using the invocation of the epistemological doubt and cramp as a justification of utmost obscurity and subjectivism (the main stylistic marks of 'postmodernism'). They agonize so much about their inability to know themselves and the Other, at any level of regress, that they no longer need to trouble too much about the Other. If everything in the world is fragmented and multiform, nothing really resembles anything else, and no one can know another (or himself), and no one can communicate, what is there to do other than express the anguish engendered by this situation in impenetrable prose?

Why waste too much time in the physical discomfort of the fieldwork situation? – the anguish, the paralysis of cognition and its inner soliloquy, can be indulged in just as well in the cafés of the capital city of the erstwhile colonial power, which had once administered the supposed fieldwork zone. Cognitive impotence and *angoisse* can be felt just as well in Paris as in the Middle Atlas. Better, really. It also requires no cumbersome or tedious negotiations for a research permit, no discomfort, no risk of malaria or snake bite. And as for style . . . why, those colonialists wrote with limpid clarity, because they dominated the world, partly by using that wicked clarity to do so. Lucid prose and the domination went hand in hand. We'll show them through our style just how anti-colonialist (and pro-feminist, for that matter) we are! And, by God, they do.

It would be exceedingly tempting to dismiss this *à outrance* subjectivism as a fad and worry no further about it – except, perhaps, to offer a sociological account of it. Rabinow, amusingly, invites us to do precisely this:[43]

One is led to consider the politics of interpretation in the academy today. . . . those are the dimensions of power to which Nietzsche exhorted us to be scrupulously attentive.

45

There can be no doubt of the existence and influence of
this type of power relation in the production of texts. . . .
My wager is that looking at the conditions under which
people are hired, given tenure, published, awarded
grants, and feted would repay the effort.

I for one am rather inclined to accept this challenge. What are
the roots of this ultra-subjectivism?

In the world's most developed countries, something around
50 per cent of the population receives higher education. The
colleges and universities which provide it are staffed by people
who are assessed in terms not merely of teaching performance
but also of intellectual creativity and originality, on the model
of an ever-growing natural science, and of great centres of
learning, where scholars find themselves on the very frontiers
of knowledge. In routine teaching establishments, and in fields
such as the humanities, not only is it not clear that there is any
cumulative development, any real 'progress', it is not always
altogether clear just what 'research' should or could aim at.
So this extensive world of university instruction is run on the
model applicable to a few centres of creative excellence, *and*
in genuinely cumulative, expanding natural sciences. There
simply must be the appearance of both profundity and originality. It is all intended to resemble scientific growth.

But what if there isn't any? May this lead to a setting up of
artificial obsolescence and rotation of fashion, characteristic of
the consumer goods industry? In the postwar era, this demand
for growth was met in American sociology by the elaboration
of a scientistic jargon, which in fact had neither sharpness of
definition, nor any real relation to reality, nor much internal
discipline, but which sounded suitably obscure and intimidat-
ing. This was followed, in anthropology, first by the 'interpretive' mood, and then by its exaggerated, self-indulgent, 'postmodernist' continuation. Each could be presented as discovery
and chance.

Two things had happened: the scientistic impulse had failed
to yield any great results, and this was eventually noticed;
and in social anthropology fieldwork became increasingly more

46

difficult and uncomfortable. Under the colonial system, the widely employed method of indirect rule preserved neat, conspicuous, ritually highlighted social structures; but in the postcolonial world the existence of archaic structures was frequently denied by the new authorities, and local administrators were hostile to extraneous researchers. Their ideology precluded the recognition of archaic structures, their interests were threatened by the presence of independent outsiders, free to report whatever they liked. The disillusion with the scientistic aspiration and the inconveniences, conceptual and political, of trying to find things out on the ground made it terribly attractive to turn to hermeneutic-relativist-subjectivism.[44] One could inspect one's own soul and its anguish at failing to find out anything (no clearance whatever is required from the Ministry of the Interior to think about yourself and indulge in hermeneutic Angst). The Language of Deep Subjectivity, especially when borrowing its terminology from the Parisian Left Bank, could be at least as dauntingly and impressively obscure as any of the erstwhile scientistic sociology. It shows that you have a mystery to reveal, an illumination to bring, in brief that you have something to teach. The Hermeneutic Way to Cultural Equality – all clusters of meaning are equal – also squarely places you amongst the political angels.

The scientism and subjectivism could even be combined. This confluence of the initial scientism and the subsequent hermeneutic subjectivism is noted by George Marcus:[45]

> there has been no shortage of works addressing what Anthony Giddens (1979) has called the central problem of social theory: the integration of action perspectives, standing for the positivist programme predominant in post-war Anglo-American social thought, with meaning perspectives, standing for the interpretive paradigm.

Just why kicking the dead dragon of colonialism some decades after his demise should earn you any medals is less than clear to me. (It should be said that Rabinow himself makes this point.[46] He rightly notes that the politics which really makes an impact is not the colonialism of yesteryear but the academic politics of today.) And originality, required for academic recognition, can be claimed: Geertz had started it all with his hermeneutic turn in anthropology, but you can claim he had not gone far enough – why, the man's work is full of references to the real world . . . does he not realize that any claims, however guarded, to such access still betray a lack of sensitivity to our predicament?

The problem of knowledge, and in particular the problem of knowing alien conceptual system, gives rise to deep and unsolved dilemmas. One can use these difficulties to castigate all those who had previously – problems or not – come back with clear and intelligible data, and present one's own unintelligibility and inward-turnedness, peppered with all the great names in the history of ideas, as so much deeper. It also takes much less work. This is part of the 'political' explanation. There is also the wider consideration that this hermeneutic awe of the Other is presented as somehow linked (indispensably?) to intercultural egalitarianism: unless you speak as we do, you are a colonialist, if not worse. It is presented as a precondition of liberation and equality. These links are spurious, but they are assiduously insinuated.

As Rabinow has invited us to offer a political explication of the current power and production state of play in the groves of academe, I modestly offer the above hypothesis, with the immodest suggestion that it might well have rather pleased the Nietzsche whom Rabinow invokes. It is a bit in his style, I like to think. It was he and Heine who saw the links between German philosophical idealism and the life situation of the German clerics and professors. But it would be a pity to leave the matter there. These at any rate may be the immediate antecedents of relativism-subjectivism; there are also deeper and more general ones and I'll return to those.

The fact that this relativism leads to sloppy research, appalling prose, much pretentious obscurity, and in any case constitutes a highly ephemeral phenomenon, destined for oblivion when the next fad arrives, is not all there is to say. What is far more important is to specify why any *relativism simply will not do*.

A curious piece, emphatically affirming a contrary view, appeared in the *American Anthropologist* in 1984[47] from the pen of the man who has indeed done so much to influence this movement and prepare its foundations, even though the movement also now aspires to transcend him – namely, Clifford Geertz. The piece is a defence of relativism against its critics, though it claims that it is not meant to be a positive endorsement of it. As such it is highly relevant for the present purpose. It is careful to describe itself as anti-anti-relativist, rather than relativist. As the double use of 'anti' is awkward, whilst I respect Geertz's wish not to be described simply as 'relativist', without however being convinced by it, I'll use the expression 'pro-relativist', without prejudice, simply as a kind of shorthand for the awkward 'anti-anti'.

The author is impatient with those who, in his view, misunderstand the situation. For instance, he pokes fun at Ian Jarvie's excellent summary of relativism – 'all assessments are . . . relative to some standard . . . and standards derive from cultures'[48] – notwithstanding the fact that Geertz himself at the end of the essay explicitly embraces relativism precisely in this form, and notwithstanding the fact that Jarvie's derivation of nihilism from this position is altogether lucid and cogent.

Jarvie's simple and unanswerable point is that if all standards are an expression of culture (and cannot be anything else), then no sense whatever can be ascribed to criticizing cultures as a whole. No standards can then conceivably exist, in terms of which this could ever be done. If standards are inescapably expressions of a culture, how could a culture be judged? Geertz seems bizarrely blind to this genuine and fully justified fear; he answers it only, apart from the sustained, contemptuous but argument-less derision, by appealing to the fact that he himself is 'no nihilist', and the (unsubstantiated) claim that real nihilists are not inspired by anthropological relativism, and the claim that something called provincialism is a worse danger than relativism.

Relativism *does* entail nihilism: if standards are inherently and inescapably expressions of something called culture, and can be nothing else, then no culture can be subjected to a standard, because (*ex hypothesi*) there cannot be a trans-cultural standard which would stand in judgement over it. No argument could be simpler or more conclusive. The fact that this entailment is valid does not mean that people must in fact, psychologically, also become nihilists if they are relativists. The argument is not refuted by the fact that our author is sympathetic to relativism *and* has his own standards which he upholds with firmness. We cannot legislate against inconsistency, and have no wish to do so. The existence of a contradiction in a given mind does not refute the argument. But there are some of us who are influenced and bothered by cogent inferences, and have some little difficulty in accepting premiss A and rejecting conclusion B, if (as most emphatically happens to be the case here) A does indeed entail B . . .

Geertz says in so many words: 'I myself find provincialism altogether the more real concern so far as what actually goes on in the world' (i.e. more of a menace than relativism). He goes on to say 'anti-relativism has largely concocted the anxiety it lives from'.[49] That is a matter of judgement, and I cannot possibly agree. There may be a fair amount of unsophisticated provincialism about, but in the groves of academe it is relativism which is all the rage.

The important intellectual contrast to the relativism defended by Geertz (though he makes out that he is merely an enemy of its enemies, and not necessarily its friend) is of course the doctrine of the Big Ditch, the idea that a great discontinuity has occurred in the life of mankind, the view that a form of knowledge exists which surpasses all others, both in its cognitive power and in its social iciness. Provincialists-absolutists are no longer among us, at least in reputable academic positions, and openly; but the idea that a major and crucial discontinuity occurs in the intellectual history of mankind – though not one that can be used to confer privileges on any one segment of mankind – is a respectable position. At least I hope it is, as I happen to hold it. Geertz singles out this view for some derision, comparing the alleged vainglory of those who are in awe of this tremendous fact with the conceit of those who based their superiority on the possession of the gatling-gun.[50]

Geertz, as it happens, is quite wrong in tracing the origin of this view. In a footnote,[51] he names a whole series of variant formulations of Big Ditch theory, and then refers with sarcasm to 'Popper, from whom all these blessings flow'. One must set the record straight here. Speaking as a card-carrying member of the Big Ditch movement, as an upholder of the Great Discontinuity thesis, I must stress that, from the viewpoint of our party, Karl Popper is a gravely defective *Parteigenosse*. It is true that his great *Open Society and Its Enemies*[52] is articulated in terms of the fundamental opposition of Closed and Open societies, the later linked to freedom and science, the former excluding both. To that extent, he has indeed given us some succour.

But it is a marked feature of Popper's thought that he fails to relate this opposition in any sustained or consistent way to other differences of social form. For one thing, he appears to believe that the essence of scientific thought (something which on his view is quite simple – namely *trial and error*) has been with us ever since the amoeba: Einstein's work does not differ from that of the amoeba, in principle.[53] So there has been no real discontinuity, no Big Ditch. He has taken little interest in attempts to investigate the social preconditions of intellectual openness, other than some rather minor and virtually shame-faced discussion of its affinity to the commercial spirit. He generally gives the strong impression that the open spirit emerges, whether in ancient Greece or *fin-de-siècle* Vienna, as a result of a kind of personal, socially disconnected heroism-cum-modesty. A brave free spirit reaffirms the ancient custom of the amoeba, questions ideas rather than protecting them, and defies the *Drang* towards closed tribalism, which has for some reason mysteriously suspended the open amoebic tradition amongst the human race.

The point about the greater danger of provincialism is interesting. A narrow failure to perceive or grasp fully the cultural diversity of the world may indeed be a greater danger in North America than elsewhere. North American society was *born* modern, and sprang from those elements in English society which contributed most to the emergence of the modern world: it was not for nothing that Max Weber chose, rather strangely, an eighteenth-century American, Benjamin Franklin, to illustrate something he wanted to say about the seventeenth-century English spirit . . .

But more than that: America's fabulous wealth and its relatively wide dispersal, the wide (though of course not complete) participation in the national cultural ideal, the egalitarianism and stress on mobility, and above all the absence of any real recollection or even any haunting smell of any *ancien régime* – all these traits make Americans, to this day, inclined to absolutize their own culture, and to equate it with the human condition as such, and hence unconsciously to treat other cultures as perversions of the rightful human condition. Individualism, egalitarianism, freedom, sustained innovation – these traits are, in the comparative context of world history, unusual, not to say eccentric; but to Americans they are part of the air they breathe, and most of them have never experienced any other moral atmosphere. The one indigenous American philosophy, Pragmatism, does in fact make experimental innovation into an inherent and external part of human cognition as such, thus showing a total blindness to its absence in most other cultures.

No wonder that Americans tend to treat these principles as universal and inherent in the human condition. The preamble to the American Declaration of Independence informs them that its truths are self-evident, and Americans tend to assume it to be so. But they are nothing of the kind: these assumptions are in fact heretical or unintelligible in most other cultures. Tourism, Junior Years Abroad, etc. perhaps haven't really eroded the American illusion. It is *this* which gives the hermeneutic message its exciting flavour in America; when Middle America at long last grasps the message, it is liable to find it novel and intoxicating, in its total inversion of old habits of thought.

There are parts of the world – e.g. Levantine ports – where

every street peddler is at home in a number of languages, and is familiar with the idiosyncrasies of a number of cultures; in such an audience, the relativist message could only produce a yawn. But in Middle America it can still come as a revelation. This shock-potential has of course been exploited to the full, and a truism – meanings are not identical in all cultures – has indeed been presented as a revelation, as something which requires arduous initiation and professional sophistication.

It is of course perfectly in order for Geertz to make it his central task to educate and correct what he sees as the provincialism of his compatriots; but even if one grants him that this provincialism is still pervasive – I wouldn't wish to pronounce on this, not being an expert on Middle America – it does not in the least justify decrying, ironizing and denouncing a sense of the danger of relativism-induced nihilism, and of calling this kind of fear – in a whole battery of sustained abuse – 'cooked-up alarms', etc. It is not in the least 'cooked up'. It is only too genuine, and his own bizarre – and, may I add, ethnocentric and insular, not to say deeply provincial – insensitivity to it does not make it any less so.

Let there be not the slightest doubt about whether Geertz is indeed a relativist, and not merely an 'anti-anti-relativist'. At the beginning of the article, he does somewhat fudge the issue, by suggesting that his own anti-anti-relativism does not commit him to relativism:[54]

In this frame, the double negative simply doesn't work in the usual way. . . . It enables one to reject something without thereby committing oneself to what it rejects. And this is precisely what I want to do with anti-relativism.

But we do not need here to appeal to the conventional use of the double negative in logic. We can gladly grant him an eccentric use of the double negation sign. (He is quite right, though he formulates it in a somewhat weird manner. 'Anti' is not a straightforward equivalent of negation. It was indeed perfectly possible, for instance, to use Geertz's own example, to be anti-McCarthyite without being pro-Communist, and without favouring that which McCarthy denounced.) We can use his own final statement in the article, which contains a very elegant definition – and unqualified endorsement – of relativism. He disparages those engaged in 'placing morality beyond culture and knowledge beyond both. This . . . is no longer possible.'

The denial of the possibility that morality could be beyond culture, and knowledge beyond both, is in fact an extremely acceptable definition of relativism, and one that I am perfectly happy to use. To deny that knowledge beyond culture is possible *is* to affirm relativism. (It is strange that he should say that it is *no longer* possible, which clearly suggests that it had once been possible. Surely, on his own premises, it could only have *seemed* possible . . . ? But let is pass.)

Let us accept the terms of reference imposed by Geertz's definition. The point is – what we desperately need is precisely a morality beyond culture, and knowledge beyond both morality *and* culture. As it happens, we do appear to possess the latter, but not the former. I am not sure whether indeed we possess morality beyond culture, but I am absolutely certain that we do indeed possess knowledge beyond both culture and morality. This, as it happens, is both our fortune and our disaster. The fact that we do so *is the central and by far the most important point about our shared social condition*: any system which denies it, such as 'interpretive anthropology', is an appalling travesty of our real situation. The existence of trans-cultural and amoral knowledge is *the* fact of our lives. I am not saying that it is *good*; but I am absolutely certain that it is a fact. It must be the starting point of any remotely adequate anthropology or social thought. But more of that in due course.

There is one possible misunderstanding which must be avoided. My insistence that relativism *must logically* lead to nihilism (irrespective of whether individuals psychologically actually make the inference, or feel its force) may give the impression that my argument is that *because* nihilism is repulsive, and because relativism entails it, *therefore* relativism must be false. Nothing of the kind is being proposed. It has never been my view that this universe is arranged for our convenience, pleasure or edification, and that repellent views may not be true. On the contrary, if anything, I am somewhat inclined to the opposite and pessimistic view, and am rather given to the suspicion that if an idea is repulsive, it is probably correct. I would not actually elevate this to the level of a logical principle, if only because on occasion one finds mutually incompatible repulsive ideas, and they cannot all of them be true at the same time. But the pessimistic assumption seems to me on the whole wiser, and the repellent nature of nihilism in no way disestablishes relativism. On the contrary: it only renders it more menacing.

In fact I do not in any way exclude the possibility that relativism is valid: perhaps, indeed, in the end we cannot establish values, and the values which guide life and inspire men are contingent, and can have no foundation other than those circular self-confirming systems of thought and sentiment we call cultures. I do not propose to set up as someone capable of settling this momentous issue. But if moral relativism *is* valid, it isn't valid as a corollary of the establishment of cognitive relativism, of the cognitive equality of all thought styles. Such an equality does *not* obtain. What is true is that (contrary to Geertz's protestations) nihilism *does* follow from such a relativism, and it could be inferred from it, were such a relativism firmly established.

But everything about the condition of mankind in our age makes it utterly plain that cognitive relativism is false. It is false because an enormous mass of social facts establishes this, and *not* because it would have disastrous consequences if true (though in fact it does have those corollaries). They might be true, but that cannot be established from the premiss of hermeneutic egalitarianism of all thought-systems, for such a premiss is not available to us. It is false.

So there *are* powerful arguments against cognitive relativism of a totally different order. One of them, perhaps the most important, is that relativism is not so much a misguided solution, as a dreadfully inadequate formulation of our *problem*. It simply and totally misdescribes our collective situation. As a characterization of the predicament and difficulties and anxiety faced by the modern mind, it is a total travesty, so strange and extreme as to make any handling of our problem impossible.

The problem situation faced by modern thought in general, and anthropology in particular, is deeply unsymmetrical and un-relativistic. Relativism assumes or postulates a symmetrical world. Culture A has its own vision of itself and of culture B, and, likewise, B has its own vision of itself and of A. The same goes for the entire range of cultures. A must not sit in judgement on B nor vice versa, nor must B see A in terms of itself. Each must learn to see the other in terms of the other's own notions (if at all), and this is, presumably, the task and achievement of the hermeneutic anthropologist, as he himself envisages it. He is to be a neutral translator, at most. That is the picture presented by relativism.

Often members of both A and B are liable to be somewhat ethnocentric, given to thinking that their own concepts capture the world as it really is, and that the Other should see himself and everything else in their own terms, and is being silly if he fails to do so. In view of all this, the hermeneutic anthropologist's first task is to cure his audience of its ethnocentric ('provincial') leanings, and to upbraid it in no uncertain terms for those leanings. This he evidently does with enormous gusto and enjoyment. He gives his audience to understand that comprehending an alien culture is dreadfully difficult, and takes a special kind of insight and sophistication, which most emphatically is not granted to everyone. This is one of the temptations to which the hermeneutic school is prone, and to which practitioners of postmodernism succumb with ecstasy, and in dreadful literary style: they become so enthusiastic and inebriated with the difficulty of explicating the Other that in the end they don't even try to reach it, but content themselves with elaborating the theme of its inaccessibility, offering a kind of initiation into a Cloud of Unknowing, a Privileged Non-Access . . . The Inaccessibility of the Other becomes a science and a mystery on its own.

But, accessible or not, the imaginary universe of our hermeneutic relativist is symmetrical. It somewhat resembles the expanding universe of the physicists, in which discrete galaxies all recede from each other, and the universe as a whole looks much the same from any given vantage point. The important thing is, indeed, that there must be no privileged vantage point. That was the ideology of colonialism. The truth is that all cultures are equal, and no single one of them has the right to judge and interpret the others in its own terms, and, above all (the ultimate horror), it must not claim that the world is correctly described in its own terms. It is this fearful symmetry which is a total and disastrous travesty of the world we live in. Anyone who endorses it cannot even begin to understand the present human condition.

The world we actually inhabit is totally different. Some two millennia and a half ago, it did perhaps more or less resemble the world the relativist likes to paint, at least in some measure: there was a multiplicity of communities, each with its own rites and legends. It would have been truly absurd to try to elevate one of them above the others, and, still more, to claim that the truth about any one of them was only to be had in the terminology of another. Such un-even-handed asymmetry would have been preposterous and pointless (though one could hardly altogether dismiss Greek thought, and the inception within it of a universally valid logic and geometry).

Then came the Axial Age, as it was christened by Karl Jaspers,[55] and reintroduced into recent discussion by S. N. Eisenstadt.[56] This means that a certain number of cultures emerged, within which the relationship between the Transcendent and the Social had become rather more tense: the Transcendent liberated itself from at least the more obvious and visible dependence on the Social, claimed to sit in judgement on it, and assumed an authority going beyond the limits of any one community, polity or ethnic group. Doctrines and theory acquired an autonomy of their own, and were not simply the liturgical accompaniment of a socially bounded ritual. The non-relativistic snake had entered the Garden of Eden, never to leave it again. It transformed us and our world: we are the heirs, willing or reluctant, sometimes both, of this transformation. Socially independent scientific truth was preceded, and presumably made possible, by socially disembodied religion.

And then, over two millennia later, a few hundred years before our own time, a terrible thing happened.

One of the post-Axial cultures was possessed, rightly or wrongly, by the idea of the uniqueness and universality of truth, of its own faith. Within it, eventually, a secular, non-religious variant of the cognitive style emerged. If Max Weber and his followers are to be believed, it owed a great deal to the orderly and unified precedent, set for it by its local religious predecessor, and would never have emerged without it. An exclusive, jealous, distant and orderly unique deity may generate a vision of the world which offers, in religious terms, a variant of or precedent for the rationalist conception of Nature and knowledge, and it may well be the precondition of its emergence. Rationalism was the continuation of exclusive monotheism by other means. This secular variant, known as natural science, had certain most remarkable attributes and consequences, as follows.

1 Its propositions and claims are translatable without loss of efficacy into any culture and any milieu.
2 In its applied or technological form, this new knowledge has totally transformed the human social condition, and the terms of reference under which mankind lives.

Previously, agrarian humanity lived in a Malthusian world in which scarcity of resources on the whole condemned men to tight, authoritarian social forms, to domination by either tyrants or cousins or both. Men were subjected to authoritarian monarchies or to ritually enforced, pervasive, demanding intimate groups, conceptualized in terms of kinship, and sanctioned by selective access to social rites. The two forms of subjection could also be combined. Scarcity of resources in relation to need and population both necessitated and facilitated a stratified humanity: men starved and suffered not at random, but in accordance with ascribed rank. Now, suddenly, resources outstrip population, and so domination becomes optional rather than mandatory. It is no longer *necessary* for anyone to starve. Social order is still indispensable, but it is no longer rendered mandatory by the need for discipline in the social queue for essentials, and it need no longer be sanctioned by the attachment of men to their place in the social queue.

3 In its internal organization, the new learning which makes the new social order possible is both cumulative and astonishingly consensual. It grows faster and faster, it does not endlessly retrace its steps or fragment arbitrarily or go round in circles (as had been the general fate of previous essays at theorizing about the world). Its practitioners *agree*, to a very remarkable extent, and they agree in the way in which they replace ideas by better ones. They agree, without being coerced into agreeing. In fact their consensus is such that one would suspect a conspiracy, were it not for the fact that it is not enforced by threats, and that they also deliver the goods, and that is something which most certainly cannot be faked.

No one quite knows just *how* it is done. It is an interesting point that science *is* consensual, but the philosophy of science is *not*. Scientists on the whole agree and converge, theoreticians of science do not. But there is no shadow of doubt *that* it is done, even if we do not know just *how* it is done.

4 This new learning respects neither the culture, nor the morality, of either the society in which it was born, or of those in which it makes itself at home by diffusion. It is, most emphatically, 'beyond culture and morality'. Alas, often it is not only *beyond*, but also *against*. One of the bitterest and most deeply felt, and alas justified, complaints against science is, precisely, that it disrupts morality. It does not, as the previous, technologically impotent (or very nearly so) learning had done, serve to underwrite social and political arrangements, and to make men feel more or less at home in the world and at ease with it, or indeed in awe of it, whilst signally failing to help control it. Past belief systems were technically spurious and morally consoling. Science is the opposite. Science markedly fails to perform such social services, and the attempts to enlist

59

it to and oblige it to perform them have failed abysmally (the year 1989 witnessed the final and dramatic collapse of the most elaborate and ambitious of such attempts). Its failure to legitimate social arrangements, and to make men feel at home in the world, is the commonest charge levelled at science. The charge is entirely valid.

This is the world we live in, for better or for worse. We have absolutely no choice in this matter. The problems we face flow precisely from these features of our world, and we cannot evade them. To pretend that we are somehow or other living in a pre-scientific and even a pre-Axial world, in which all meanings-systems are equal, in order to provide titillation for Middle America, and to indulge in a rite of expiation for a vanishing hegemony, is simply absurd. The sooner this nonsense stops the better.

The pro-relativism (or anti-anti-relativism, if you insist) Geertz commends is in fact a marked expression of that very provincialism which it would wish to combat. The provincial absolutist, having tumbled to the discovery that his culture is simply *a* culture, amongst others, and not simply a natural, self-evident reflection of the Nature of Things, becomes intoxicated with the idea of plurality of visions. Feeling somewhat guilty about being richer and more powerful than others, he links his well-meaning, benign cultural 'hermeneutic' egalitarianism to a repudiation of logical as well as political dominance. But in so doing, he is in fact repeating his earlier ethnocentrism in a new and bizarre form. In his eagerness to apologize for his previous innocence, he adopts a new form of it, and imagines away the dramatic, perhaps tragic, asymmetry of our world. The world we live in is defined, above all, by the existence of a unique, unstable and powerful system of knowledge of nature, and its corrosive, unharmonious relationship to the other clusters of ideas ('cultures') in terms of which men live. *This* is our problem. The make-believe, spurious and invented symmetric vogue is the ultimate provincialism, and renders genuine thought impossible.

But why has all this happened? One particular style of

knowledge has proved so overwhelmingly powerful, economically, militarily, administratively, that all societies have had to
make their peace with it and adopt it. Some have done it more
successfully than others, and some more willingly or more
quickly than others; but all of them have had to do it, or
perish. Some have retained more, and some less, of their
previous culture.

The postulation of this kind of completely indisputable
asymmetry has nothing whatever to do with a racist, or any
other, glorification of one segment of humanity over another.
It is a style of knowledge and its implementation, not any
category of personnel, which is being singled out as symmetry-
defying. That style of knowledge did of course have to emerge
somewhere and at some time, and to this extent it certainly
has historical links with a particular tradition or culture. It
emerged in one social context, but it is clearly accessible to all
humanity, but endorses none; and it does rather look as if it
were *more* accessible to some segments of mankind amongst
whom it had *not* sprung up spontaneously. Its greatest elective
affinity need not be, and probably isn't, with its place of origin.
The first industrial and scientific nation is not, at present, at
the top of the First Industrial Division. It sometimes looks as
if it were struggling in the relegation zone. This is a curious
and important fact, one which had become conspicuous in the
course of this century.

So the conditions which have favoured its emergence are
not necessarily the same as those which favour its subsequent
development: in the late twentieth century, industrialism is
doing rather less well in its place of origin than it is in countries
which failed to give birth to it, and were perhaps rather
unlikely ever to do so. It is not clear which of the conditions
surrounding its birth were crucial, and which were merely
accidental and irrelevant, and presumably the crucial ones
might have come together in other places and at other times.
But above all, it is absolutely clear that the asymmetry-engen-
dering powerful form of cognition is not the prerogative of
any one human group. So it does not, in this sense, give rise
to any ranking of human groups.

The great asymmetry has as it were two dimensions. On the one hand, it is *one particular* post-Axial cognitive style which has, by some means or other, trumped all the others, when judged by the pragmatic criterion of technological efficacy, but also by criteria such as precision, elaboration, elegance, and sustained and consensual growth. On the other hand, looking at the diversity of human activities, this great power only really seems to work in certain fields – natural sciences, technology. In other spheres, the understanding of society and of culture for instance, its application has no doubt somewhat raised our level of information and sophistication, but one is hardly tempted to speak of a breath-taking revolution, one which changes the very terms of reference within which we live our lives. This is perhaps one of the factors which attracts people to hermeneuticism: it promises an explanation of this failure, perhaps a remedy of it, or a replacement of the aspiration of applying science to man at all, by one which is both more attractive and less likely to disappoint.

But this enormous double asymmetry – one kind of knowledge works, and all the others do not (or, rather, not with remotely the same effectiveness), and it works in one sphere of life and not in others, at any rate so far – provides the background against which we must live and think. The hermeneutically formulated doctrine of symmetry denies this, and thereby makes any realistic thought impossible. One cannot think straight if one begins by closing one's eyes to reality. The hermeneutic equality of all systems of meaning precludes us from even *asking*, let alone from answering, the question concerning why the world is so very unsymmetrical, why there is such a desperate wish to emulate the success of one kind of cognition, and why there is a discrepancy between fields in which the success is achieved and those in which it is absent. The real and greatest objection to relativism is not that it proposes a false solution (though it does), but that it prevents us from even seeing and formulating our problem.

The wilful and sometimes flamboyant unwillingness to face the central fact of our time – justifying this by the facile argument that men live through cultural meanings, cultural meanings are ultimate and self-sustaining, therefore all cultures are cognitively equal, therefore the central fact of our time could not have happened, even if it did – is one of the main sins of hermeneutic symmetricism, but not the only one. Another important one is the permanent, deeply inherent bias of such thought towards idealism. By this I mean the undervaluing of coercive and economic constraints in society, and the overvaluing of conceptual ones. This is curious, in as far as hermeneutists (at any rate in the post–1945 world) tend to be to the left, or at any rate often opposed to and critical of the established order. You would expect them to be highly sensitive to coercive and economic forms of constraint, and the way in which the rulers of a society monopolize power and economic levers so as to retain and enhance their own position. You might expect them to be aware of the way in which political and economic coercion underwrites and imposes meanings, rather than focussing mainly or even exclusively on the way in which meanings are used to reinforce political and economic inequality. But hermeneutists do not seem to be very interested in political and economic structures: it is domination by symbols and discourse which really secures and retains their attention. They are enormously sensitive to the manner in which concepts *constrain*, and less than attentive to other, and perhaps more important, forms of coercion. Their attitude engenders a selective sensitivity which in effect ignores those other constraints, or even by implication denies their existence. If we live in a world of meanings, and meanings exhaust the world, where is there any room for coercion through the whip, gun, or hunger? The cosy world of the well-heeled scholar is allowed to stand in for the harsh world outside.

Indisputably, it is the case that concepts do constrain. Concepts, the range of available ideas, all that is suggested by a given language, and all that which is inexpressible in it are part of the machinery of social control in any given society. What is *not* obvious is just how important a part conceptual constraint plays, when compared with political or economic pressures. There is no reason to suppose that the same answer applies at all times and in all places.

What is obvious is that conceptual constraint is not the *only* mechanism operative. Russian society, for instance, was transformed radically between 1916 and 1918, as a result of the events of 1917; or German society between 1944 and 1946, as a result of the defeat of 1945. Power changed hands; the identity of those who could kill, and those liable to be killed, altered radically. But there is no reason to suppose that the internal conceptual world of the average Russian or German changed so very much, or quite as quickly, during the same period: it probably changed a bit under the impact of events, but it is unlikely, for the majority of people, to have changed profoundly. They could hardly transform their ideas quite so rapidly. But the society, and above all its authority structure, did change utterly. Obviously, the profound shifts in the authority structures cannot be attributed to the rather minor (at most) and tentative initial changes in the systems of meaning. It is obvious that these very dramatic alterations were produced by a transfer of the means of physical coercion from one set of hands to another, as a result of a revolution in one case, or of a lost war in another, and *not* by some semantic transformation. What mattered was who held the gun, and who did not. To suppose the contrary is to indulge in an absurd form of idealism. It is only the abstract, unhistorical formulation of the hermeneutic doctrine which obscures its utter silliness.

Hermeneutists tend to slide over quietly from the perfectly valid perception that concepts do constrain, to the totally indefensible idealist doctrine, or rather operational assumption, that *only* concepts constrain. Why? Could it be the intellectual's conceit and the pleasure at the thought that his own tools, i.e. ideas, are really that which controls the social order, and guides the pattern of history? I have always suspected that this was one of the roots of sociological idealism, from Hegel onwards. Or is it the fact that conceptual structures are so much more easily accessible, especially in the post-colonial period? By a supreme irony, it is precisely the social condition which was actually *produced* by the asymmetry of cognitive power, the disruption of traditional societies, the pervasive cultural miscegenation (noted by Geertz when he comments on the tangled situation faced by contemporary anthropologists), which appear to impel some anthropologists into the 'hermeneutic' mode: social structures have become so tangled and complex as to be very hard to grasp. But this does not mean that they do not exist, or are reducible to systems of meaning.

It doesn't mean that objective structures do not exist or are not important. The post-colonial state is often an ideological one, committed to absurd pretensions concerning its own society – tribalism has been overcome, antagonistic classes are no longer in existence, and irredentist minorities do not exist, having affectionately embraced the dominant group. The new district officer is in fact very insecure, performing a delicate balancing act between local pressures and the intrigues of the hierarchy of which he is a member, and whose membership confers great privileges on him, which he is anxious to retain at all cost. The last thing he wants is a foreign investigator nosing about in his territory, undermining his authority by being blatantly independent of it – because he cannot be stopped from returning to his home society, and visiting whomever he pleases – thereby putting the official in danger, by eventually reporting that tribalism is rife, that class differences are enormous and acutely felt, and that the ethnic minority is sullenly discontented. As he cannot be allowed to establish and report all this, obstacles are put in his way.

So the much hampered investigator may turn, with regret or joy as the case may be, but in any case without much of an alternative, to the systems of meanings, which he can make up for himself (especially if his book consists largely of reflections concerning how very difficult it is to apprehend and articulate them, or to communicate them again when he has secured them, and how deep his anguish is whilst enduring this condition). At worst, he may choose to focus on one special informant, whom he can take along to some place where the district officer cannot interfere. There is an old theory to the effect that American anthropologists were *cultural* because it was a matter of recording the culture of Amerindians, whose political structure didn't matter much anyway, whilst the British and French anthropologists were *social*, because they worked in empires deploying indirect rule, in which local structures were quite important. Indirect rule had meant depriving the local rajah or emir of some of his power, but encouraging him to augment and accentuate his pomp and ritual, thus rendering the ritually accentuated structure all the more visible. If this is so, de-colonization has certainly swung the balance of attractiveness in favour of the cultural and against the social, by obscuring the latter and making its investigation perilous, so that there is indeed a link between decolonization and the hermeneutic twist, though not exactly the one normally invoked.

Another important factor is probably methodological. The hermeneutists have forged a tool and they must use it, and they have an interest in no rival tools being indispensable. Interpretation can, on its own, seize systems of meaning, but it simply cannot on its own seize political, economic or any other objective structures. The same system of meanings may be compatible with any number of power or wealth structures, and so cannot tell you which of them is actually operative. All this being so, in the interest of deploying his favourite, or indeed unique, tool, the hermeneutist will in practice play down the importance of these other, non-conceptual elements, or maintain that they are but the effect or artefact or reflection of those elements, without any real independent existence. In other words, he will adopt an idealist position, though one expressed in ultra-modern, semantic terminology. Hermeneutics is the modern name of idealism.

These are sins enough. The hermeneutist stance, whether in its earlier and relatively moderate formulation, or in its more extreme 'postmodernist' form, diminishes the sensitivity of those who uphold it to the central problem of our time, and prejudges various factual issues involved in it; and it impels its adepts to offer accounts of social orders which are, without any good evidence for such a conclusion, heavily weighted in the direction of an idealist interpretation. The song and dance about symbolic domination in the end inevitably obscures the reality of other, perhaps more important forms of coercion.

There is a further and somewhat ironic charge to be made

against the postmodernist and 'interpretive' fashions. For all the centrality attributed to 'meaning', for all the fuss made of it, this style of inquiry does not in fact advance our understanding of the nature and role of meaning in life, but, if anything, retards it. 'Meaning' is of course a difficult thing to investigate: it is too all-pervasive. Any object, literally anything, has to be identified, characterized, before it can even be thought about; but to attribute characteristics to something is to deploy one's 'meanings'. Meaning is there right at the start, ready to trip us up and highlight the circularity of any procedure we adopt.

However, notwithstanding this kind of difficulty, there are questions to be asked, inquiries to be undertaken. But 'interpretive' anthropology tends, strangely enough, to take the notion and nature of meaning for granted, as given, ultimate. The wilder developments of this trend use the notion of meaning more as part of a technique for intoxication, excitement and befuddlement than as a starting point for serious thought. There are important questions concerning typologies of meaning, concerning which meanings may be culturally private and which, by contrast, stretch across cultural boundaries, the criteria for establishing this, and so on. There is room for a generative grammar of meanings. What meanings are mandatory, and why? – and which are optional? These are fascinating and difficult issues. But it is idle to expect some kind of illumination or advance concerning these problems when the text one is dealing with appears to be intent on whipping its reader – and the author, presumably – into a frenzy of excitement and perplexity, with more than a touch of guilt concerning the fact that, once upon a time, clarity and uniqueness of meaning and the striving for objectivity were linked to political domination, or the suppression of women . . . and that the subject–object distinction in writing reappears, however hard we try to obscure it, so that we can always end up with the joys of guilt.

To say all this is of course not to deny the basic premises from which the whole position grew (by uncritical exaggeration). It is certainly true that the meanings prevalent in any one culture are not, all of them, immediately and easily translatable into those of another, and sometimes are not translatable at all; that identifying those meanings presupposes familiarity with context; and that meanings play an important but variable role (the extent of which, however, is not to be prejudged in advance of specific inquiry) in maintaining a given social order. All this is true, though not exactly original. Anthropologists have practised 'interpretive' techniques as they have spoken prose: it *was* their prose. They just didn't make quite such a song and dance about it. Geertz himself quotes passages from Evans-Pritchard, whose limpid lucidity he derides, showing that he equated the grasping of local concepts with the understanding of a society.[57] So what is new?

Geertz's anti-anti-relativism essay makes light of the perils of relativism. But alas one is left with the strong impression that it is not, as he claims, that he has seen through the spuriousness of the menace, and has unmasked a paper dragon, but, rather, that he has simply failed to see the problem. If knowledge and morality are inherently bounded by or rooted in culture, what happens in a Tower of Babel situation, when cultures are in rapid flux and so intermixed that one cannot tell where one begins and another ends (a complexity which, in other contexts, he himself stresses)? If that is how things stand (and they do), but there is no anchorage outside culture, the only option left is a dismal relativism. Maybe this is indeed so, at any rate in some fields; but it is absurd to pretend that it does not constitute a problem, and that it constitutes a self-induced anxiety.

The fact that an alien culture – or even a nearby sub-culture – may have meanings not immediately intelligible to the outside observer, who has to acquire before he can 'understand', is an old truism. If such 'interpretive' investigation is combined with observation of interculturally public structures – coercion, sustenance – there is nothing new. What gives interpretive anthropology its air of originality is the hint that such interpretation is everything there is to be done, or, at any rate, that it is very, very central. In the exaggerated and hysterical form this takes when it becomes 'postmodernism', it turns into a kind of witch-hunt or exorcism or purification of any vestige of an interfering or dominant observer with pretensions to objectivity, a self-excoriation made even more exciting by blissful confessions of ultimate failure.

Either/or: either there are objective facts as well as meaning-explications, or there are not. If there are, where's the novelty? It is only to be found in the stylistic packaging. But if the claim is that there are no objective facts, then it is simply false. You cannot investigate idiosyncratic meanings without placing them in the context of *nature as seen by our scientific culture*, and, in particular, in the context of the shocking inequalities of power of diverse cognitive styles. These belated decolonizers-after-the-event, so touchy about inequalities of power, seem strangely insensitive to the most important one of them all.

In practice, they tend to obscure the issue of the relative role of meanings and external facts. For instance, the main thrust of Geertz's *Negara*[58] is that the Balinese state was a theatre which conveyed meanings to its spectators, and thus should not be confused or identified with the other kind of state, which coerces its subjects into paying taxes. That is what the sustained argument hammers home. But if you read the small print, you learn that, after all, it would not have worked, even on Bali, had not the state, theatrical or not, also possessed the ability to coerce. So in the end we return to where we had started . . .

Or again, in the collective volume we have used as our postmodernist text, Rabinow, rightly urging his colleagues to look at academic 'corridor politics' rather than shouting about an anti-colonialism which no longer concerns them, observes so as to encourage them to do a bit of brave unmasking:[59]

> We know that one of the most common tactics of an elite group is to refuse to discuss − to label as vulgar or uninteresting − issues that are uncomfortable for them.

Note the confident 'we know'. Note also, however, that what we are offered here is a cross-cultural generalization, cutting across cultural idiosyncrasies of meaning, claiming to convey an objective, extraneous, local-meaning-independent truth. So, it would seem, such a thing is possible after all, at any rate when used to excoriate objectivists? But if it is, ought we not to get more discussion of the boundaries of such ordinary sociological, objective fact or tendency, and those elusive manifestations of the Other which can only be approached by postmodernist – what was it – heteroglossia . . . ?

Muddles and incoherences of this kind abound in the work. 'Interpretivism' and pro-relativism have prepared the ground, and this is the harvest.

To sum up: human societies are a complex interaction of external factors – coercion, production – and of internal meanings. That much is not in doubt. The precise nature of that interaction cannot be prejudged prior to inquiry, in favour of the predomination of semantic or 'cultural' elements. The major fact about the world as it is now constituted is that it is going through a crucial and fundamental transition, as a result of a profound and not properly understood asymmetry between one distinct cultural style and all others.

Postmodernism is a movement which, in addition to contingent flaws – obscurity, pretentiousness, faddiness, showmanship, cultural name-dropping – commits major errors in the method it recommends: its penchant for relativism and preferential attention to semantic idiosyncrasy blind it to the non-semantic aspect of society, and to the immensely important, absolutely pervasive asymmetry in cognitive and economic power in the world situation.

The relativism to which it aspires does not have, and cannot have, any kind of programme, either in politics or even in inquiry. For one thing, it is an affectation: those who propound it, or defend it against its critics, continue, whenever facing any serious issue in which their real interests are engaged, to act on the non-relativistic assumption that one particular vision is cognitively much more effective than others. Though admittedly practitioners of 'postmodernism' go very far in the direction of abandoning inquiry and theory and replacing them with an attempt actually to bring in the object itself, the Meaning of the Other, by making the object speak for himself, in the end cannot but revert to an inquiry which sets the object in the context of a world as conceived by the one dominant, 'scientific' culture.

But relativism is simply not viable as a social or political attitude. For one thing, it offends against the very cultures whose equality it wishes to establish by 'hermeneutics': *they* are eager to acquire the technological power, and, for another thing, some of them at least (those prone to 'fundamentalism') would vehemently, and rightly, repudiate any attempt to reinterpret their own convictions in a relativist spirit. They mean what they believe. For another thing, relativism falls foul of a fact about our world which, in other contexts, it itself invokes: the tangled unstable over-lapping nature of 'cultures'. We cannot advise people to do in Rome as the Romans do, when Rome no longer has stable or unique borders.

Coming to terms with the global disruption caused by the dominance of one cognitive and technological style is not going to be easy, and it certainly won't be done here. But facile relativism will not help. It is an affectation, specially attractive amongst the more naïve provincials in privileged cultures, who suppose that this inversion of their previous viewpoint will help them, all at once, to atone for their privilege, understand others and themselves, and comprehend our shared predicament. It is, alas, not that easy.

Postmodernism as such doesn't matter too much. It is a fad which owes its appeal to its seeming novelty and genuine obscurity, and it will pass soon enough, as such fashions do. But it is a specimen of relativism, and relativism does matter. Relativism isn't objectionable because it entails moral nihilism (which it *does*); moral nihilism may be hard to escape in any case. It is objectionable because it leads to *cognitive* nihilism, which is simply false, and also because it possibly misrepresents the way in which we actually understand societies and cultures. It denies or obscures tremendous differences in cognition and technical power, differences which are crucial for the understanding of current developments of human society. A vision which obscures that which matters most *cannot* be sound.

THE CHARACTERS

A good impasse drama can, like Sartre's *Huis Clos*, have three characters, linked to each other in a painful, unstable, but inescapable stale-mate. Two have already been introduced. They are grossly incommensurate in scale and importance. Muslim fundamentalism is an enormously simple, powerful, earthy, sometimes cruel, absorbing, socially fortifying movement, which gives a sense of direction and orientation to millions of men and women, many of whom live lives of bitter poverty and are subject to harsh oppression. It enables them to adjust to a new anonymous mass society by identifying with the old, long-established High Culture of their own faith, and explaining their own deprivation and humiliation as a punishment for having strayed from the true path, rather than a consequence of never having found it; a disruption and disorientation is thus turned into a social and moral ascension, an attainment of identity and dignity.

Postmodernism, by contrast, is a tortuous, somewhat affected fad, practised by at most some academics living fairly sheltered lives; large parts of it are intelligible only and at most (and often with difficulty) to those who are fully masters of the nuances of three or four abstruse academic disciplines, and much of it is not intelligible to anyone at all. But it happens to be the currently fashionable form of relativism, and relativism as such is an important intellectual option, and one which will continue to haunt us, even if the form it assumes will vary – probably with great speed – with the rapid turn-over of academic modes. Relativism was approached through its current avatar in the interests of a certain concreteness.

And yet, though so very incomparable, the two specimens chosen do provide a neat contrast in the logic of their ideas. First, a simple and uncompromising monotheism, maintaining that God has made His Will easily accessible and known to the world and that His Will is to be implemented, and to constitute the only possible base of a uniquely just and legitimate social order. An absolute Authority, severely external to this world and its various cultures, dictates Its Will to Its Creation: and that transcendent Will derives its legitimacy precisely from its unsullied, extraneous and absolute origin. The firmness, simplicity and intelligibility of the doctrine gives it dignity. Millions find it satisfying to live under its rules: that must signify something.

Next, there is a movement which denies the very possibility of extraneous validity and authority. Admittedly, it is specially insistent in this denial, when the contrary affirmation of such external validation comes from fellow-members, non-relativists *within their own society*. Relativist pudeur and ex-colonial guilt expiation on the other hand inhibit stressing the point to members of *other* cultures. The absolutism of *others* receives favoured treatment, and a warm sympathy which is very close to endorsement.

Knowledge or morality outside culture is, it claims, a chimera: each culture must roll its own knowledge and morality. Meanings are incommensurate, meanings are culturally constructed, and so all cultures are equal. Cross-cultural or cross-semantic investigation is only possible if the dignity and equality of the 'other' culture is respected. If it were characterized and dissected with lucidity and confidence, this would constitute at the very least an implied devaluation of it. So it must be studied with tremulous obscurity, with confused and contradictory approaches. So obscurity is turned into a sign, not merely of putative depth, but of intercultural respect and abstention from domination.

The first of these two movements is profoundly asymmetrical in its vision of global ideological situation: there is no God but God. All other gods and prophets are false, though a severely limited shortlist of religions of the Book may be accorded the status of protected (though in the past also humiliated) clients. Idolaters are, at least in principle, according to the formal and unrepudiated version of the creed, to be given the choice of conversion or the sword. It would, one fears, have availed them little to have squealed that their idolatrous meanings are as legitimate as any other, because it has been definitively established by most prestigious Western academics that all meanings are equal, all cultures are self-validating, and so they ought not to be put to the sword. The executioner would not have been made to relent by a quote from Wittgenstein. In fact, forcible conversions of idolaters have not been in evidence, for whatever reason; the fundamentalists have stopped short of this. But condemnations to death for apostasy have occurred (though they have not been carried out); one of them, notoriously, against an apostate resident outside the normally recognized jurisdiction of the authority passing the verdict.

The relationship of these two characters in the drama to each other is interesting. The relativists-hermeneutists are really very eager to display their universal, ecumenical tolerance and comprehension of alien cultures. The more alien, the more shocking and disturbing to the philistines, to those whom they deem to be the provincialists of their own society, the better. Very, very much the better, for the more shocking the other, the more does this comprehension highlight the superiority of the enlightened hermeneutist within his own society. The harder the comprehension, the more repellent the object destined for hermeneutic blessing, the greater the achievement, the illumination and the insight of the interpretive postmodernist. However, our hermeneutist has to pussyfoot a bit around the fact that those whom he would so eagerly tolerate and understand are not always quite so tolerant themselves. The relativist endorses the absolutism of others, and so his relativism entails an absolutism which also contradicts it. Let us leave him with that problem: there is no way out of it.

The fundamentalists, on the other hand, are not very much concerned with our relativists. I doubt whether they give them a great deal of thought. What they have noticed is that the society which harbours hermeneutists, as it harbours so much else (it can afford it), is pervaded by pluralism, doubt, half-heartedness and an inability to take its own erstwhile faith literally and practise it to the full. They are not quite clear whether they despise it for its tolerance, or rebuke it for not being tolerant enough, notably of their own intransigence: they are liable to be pervaded by both these sentiments in turn. Those Muslim scholars resident in the West who endorsed the death sentence for apostasy and blasphemy on a Muslim novelist both despise the host society for its eclectic tolerance, and yet resent its unwillingness to endorse or tolerate their own imposition of a severe law on their co-religionist.

Of course, this is viewing it in the round. There are naturally great variations in detail. There are some amongst them who uphold the faith in a personally tolerant and rational manner, who attend to the arguments of those who do not share their premises, and prefer to conduct a rational discussion, rather than simply exclude them in virtue of their point of intellectual departure.

THE THIRD MAN

There is a third position in this game or drama. There is a position which shares something with each of the two previous protagonists, but it is also endowed with features profoundly distinguishing it from them. What is it?

It is a position which, like that of the religious fundamentalists, is firmly committed to the denial of relativism. It is committed to the view that there *is* external, objective, culture-transcending knowledge: there *is* indeed 'knowledge beyond culture'. All knowledge must indeed be articulated in some idiom, but there are idioms capable of formulating questions in a way such that answers are no longer dictated by the internal characteristics of the idiom or the culture carrying it but, on the contrary, by an independent reality. The ability of cognition to reach beyond the bounds of any one cultural cocoon, and attain forms of knowledge valid for *all* – and, incidentally, an understanding of nature leading to an exceedingly powerful technology – constitutes *the* central fact about our shared social conditions.

This position, on the other hand, also does have something in common with our relativists: it does not believe in the availability of a substantive, final, world-transcending *Revelation*. It does believe in the existence of knowledge which transcends *culture*, and it is also committed to the mundane origin of knowledge and its fallible status; but it firmly repudiates the very possibility of *Revelation*. It does not allow any cultures to validate a part of itself with final authority, to decree some substantive affirmation to be privileged and exempt from scrutiny.

In terms of its social situation, this viewpoint is also located somewhere mid-way between the other two. It cannot claim to constitute the avowed and systematized faith of millions; nor can it, in all honesty, claim to sustain great masses of ordinary people, and to be easily intelligible to them, and speak in terms which make sense to men face to face with the harsh realities of daily life, and to support them through painful ordeals.

On the other hand, it is certainly more than a passing academic fad. Sketched out at first in the course of the Scientific Revolution in the seventeenth century, and worked out in detail in the eighteenth, the position which might be called Enlightenment Secular Fundamentalism has become the unwritten, but widely recognized code of cognitive conduct of many, though not all, scholars of scientific-industrial civilization. Philosophers know how to spell it out, though by no means all of them subscribe to it at present. Recently it has been out of fashion with many. It is moderately easy to formulate it, though not perhaps with complete precision, yet exceedingly hard to establish its authority.

How can this position both deny the possibility of Revelation from Outside and yet affirm extraneous, culture-transcending knowledge? This is indeed the crucial question. First, a confession.

Suppose that, *per impossibile*, I had roughly the kind of intellectual equipment which I do have, but no positive acquaintance with this world at all: endowed with more or less the kind of dispositions and expectations which I actually possess, but without any specific information, notably in the fields which specially interest me, those of human societies and his-

76

tory. In other words, allow me a variant of the recently fashionable game of the 'Veil of Ignorance'. Suppose then that, in this condition, someone told me that indeed there was a planet Earth, fairly populous, with its inhabitants sub-divided into a variety of societies and cultures. Suppose further that I was then asked to guess what the situation was on Earth, especially in this matter of cognition and belief.

My answer, based on guesswork and merely a priori plausibility (*ex hypothesi*, I have no actual information), would probably be closer to the picture which some milder hermeneutic relativists in fact also offer, though I hope I'd state it in more lucid prose; at any rate I'd make it my starting point. Having been told that there is cultural diversity on Earth, I would hazard the guess that each culture has its own distinctive conceptual way of handling and classifying things, that each has its own norms of cognitive and moral propriety, that each culture internally is a more or less coherent system, but that, though partial communication between them is possible when carried out by skilful, sensitive poets-anthropologists (no other kind being conceivable), it simply makes no sense to ask which of the various cultural conceptual schemes is the 'correct one', and that to judge any one of them in terms of another would be a solecism, and one which a civilized, sophisticated person should avoid. This would be my guess, and I also think that my answer would not be too bad a first guess concerning our Earth as it was prior to the Axial Age, prior to some date located in the first half of the first millennium BC.

This is what I would *expect*. It seems to me most reasonable to have an expectation of that kind.

But, as it happens, I am not an outsider to this world, nor devoid of all knowledge concerning its internal organization and history. I have a fair amount of information concerning these matters, having been about for quite some time, and having taken a sustained professional interest, for what that's worth, in them. And the single most striking, indeed shattering, fact about the world I live in is that real, culture-transcending knowledge *does* exist. I might never have believed it possible a priori, because I am quite familiar with all the powerful

77

arguments purporting to show that no culture-transcending knowledge is possible; and I am also fairly at home in philosophy, and familiar with the quite strong arguments showing that no knowledge at all is possible. So, in the absence of overwhelming contrary evidence, I would respect the conclusions of those quite cogent and impressive arguments. I would expect mankind to live in a set of self-sustaining quasi-cognitive cultural cocoons, each of them endorsing its own values and practices, and ignoring or damning those of others. I might well share David Hume's preference for traditional cultures based on story and ritual and tolerant of diversity, as against scriptural doctrinal religions eager to convert all rivals. I would expect each culture to be possessed of a fair amount of practical knowledge enabling it to survive in its particular environment, but would not expect it to be capable of extending this cognitive bridgehead so as to attain really comprehensive, powerful, cumulative understanding of nature ('science'). In fact, mankind did for a long time live in precisely such a condition.

But that is not the situation we actually do find. We happen to live in a world in which one style of knowledge, though born of one culture, is being adapted by all of them, with enormous speed and eagerness, and is disrupting many of them, and is totally transforming the milieu in which men live.

This is simply a fact. I am not starry-eyed in the face of it, for the consequences of this overwhelming fact are a pretty mixed lot, some exciting, but many of them terrifying. But I try to work out what it presupposes and implies, because much of it *is* rather mysterious, and all of it is important: no one really knows just how and why this unbelievably powerful cognitive style works, and no one knows exactly how it emerged, and no one knows what its eventual social implications will be. Its existence, however, is not in doubt, though its general nature, *and* explanation, and consequences, all remain highly contentious. Philosophy has for the past three centuries been largely concerned with this issue (though its practitioners have seldom been fully clear about it, least of all of late), and sociological theory was largely born of this set of questions.

To my mild astonishment, I find that, centred on the society most affected by the transformation of life by genuine knowledge, a pervasive movement has emerged which denies, not any answer I might give to these problems – God knows I have no confidence in any answer I may offer to this question – but, rather, one which actually denies the existence of *problem* itself, and which claims to see a world in which this issue doesn't even arise.

My astonishment is mild, because bizarre though this phenomenon is intellectually, it is not so very surprising socially. The sheer superiority of the new style of cognition, and the manner in which it disrupts the web of belief in the society within which it appears, has produced a whole series of reactions against it, which can generically be called 'romanticism'. The more securely a society is in possession of the new knowledge, the more totally it is committed to its use and is pervaded by it, the more it is liable to produce thinkers who turn and bite the hand which feeds them. Precariously modernizing societies, with an uncertain grip on the new benefits, are perhaps a little less liable to indulge in an orgy of science-bashing, though it is not unknown; and, also, they are much less liable to be endowed with the spare intellectual equipment required to do so. But a really rich industrial country, in which the new conceptual plumbing is installed throughout and functions almost flawlessly, silently and discreetly, can and does afford the luxury of denouncing and renouncing it all, of returning to the old simplicities, or at any rate proclaiming that the old simplicities and the new luxuries are much of a muchness, and in any case that one must not value one above the other, that each is to be judged by its own standards, and that no standard can stand beyond culture, and all cultures constitute their own justifications . . . Relativism, basically an affectation, is most attractive in places where it is least relevant, places which have benefited most from the *a*symmetrical nature of knowledge.

RATIONALIST FUNDAMENTALISM

Enlightenment Rationalist Fundamentalism, of which I am a humble adherent, repudiates any substantive revelations. It repudiates that substantive absolutization so characteristic of some post-Axial world religions which attribute an extra-mundane and trans-cultural standing and authority to given substantive affirmations and values; and, to this extent, at any rate, it resembles our relativists.

But whilst absolutizing no *substantive* conviction – no affirmation that this or that absolutely must be *thus* – it does absolutize some formal, one might say procedural, principles of knowledge, and perhaps also (especially in its Kantian version) of moral valuation. We must proceed in a certain way in our inquiries; and this principle is then certainly trans-cultural – it is beholden to no culture – and even, in a sense, transmundane. Whatever world we might find ourselves in, there could be only one way to go about exploring it!

Absolutist and non-relativistic in procedure, and permanently *attentiste* rather than relativist in its substantive, first-order conviction: that is the basic stance of Enlightenment Rationalist Fundamentalism.

The precise details of scientific method, of the cognitive procedure discovered in the course of the Scientific Revolution and codified by the Enlightenment, continue to be contentious. But in rough outline, it is possible to specify them: there are no privileged or a priori *substantive* truths. (This, at one fell swoop, eliminates the sacred from the world.) All facts and all observers are equal. There are no privileged Sources or Affirmations, and all of them can be queried. In inquiry, all facts and all features are separable: it is *always* proper to inquire whether combinations could not be other than what had previously been supposed. In other words, the world does not arrive as a package-deal – which is the customary manner in which it appears in traditional cultures – but piecemeal. Strictly speaking, though it *arrives* as a package-deal, it is dismembered by thought.

Cultures are package-deal worlds; scientific inquiry, by

contrast, requires atomization of evidence. No *linkages* escape scrutiny. Empiricist theory of knowledge claimed that information actually arrives in tiny packages (which is false as a descriptive account); but the lesson learnt was that it should be treated *as if* it was so broken up. Such breaking up of clusters fosters critical revaluation of world-pictures. This re-examination of all associations destabilizes all cognitive *anciens régimes*. Moreover, the laws to which this world is subject are symmetrical. This levels out the world, and thereby 'disenchants' it, in the famous Weberian expression.

This is the vision. Note again, it desacralizes, disestablishes, disenchants everything substantive: *no* privileged facts, occasions, individuals, institutions or associations. In other words, no miracles, no divine interventions and conjuring performances and press conferences, no saviours, no sacred churches or sacramental communities. All hypotheses are subject to scrutiny, all facts open to novel interpretations, and all facts subject to symmetrical laws which preclude the miraculous, the sacred occasion, the intrusion of the Other into the Mundane.

But what is perhaps absolutized and made exempt is the method itself. And the method leaves its shadow on the world: it engenders an orderly, symmetrical Nature. The orderliness of inquiry leaves its shadow, and appears as an orderly, unique nature. This is the proper sense which is to be attributed to the Kantian doctrine that we 'make' our world: an orderly, systematic, law-bound Nature is really the shadow of our cognitive procedure. Kant's Copernican Revolution consisted of saying: there is *no* way of proving that the world must be like that (which would thereby vindicate the possibility of science, by guaranteeing that the world must be eligible for successful inquiry). What we *can* show is that the world must appear to be such, if we think in a certain way – and we *do*. It was left for the sociologist Weber to complement the philosopher Kant and to show that only *some* of us think that way – and to add that the practical success of this style of thought is inducing all of mankind to adopt this style, at least in some measure.

Does the Method, the insights it embodies, claim

81

transcendence? I believe it does, twice over. There are two kinds (at least) of 'transcendence': being beyond and outside a culture or any culture, and being beyond and outside this world. The epistemology of the Enlightenment in effect makes both claims. The cognitive strategy adopted, which requires the breakup of data into elements and their subsumption under general laws, would be the correct strategy in *any* world. Similarly, this is what knowledge as such is like, rather than being merely the cognitive aspect of this or that culture. Pre-Enlightenment cultures are of course endowed with their own forms of cognition, and their styles differ from the one here described; but this is precisely why they were so feeble technically, and why they are being swept aside so brutally, once knowledge-proper has seen the light of day or of history.

The actual writings of the Enlightenment weren't always fully lucid and consistent. The Enlightenment was eager to deny religious transcendence and to affirm that everything was to be found within a single, orderly System of Nature.[60] But at the same time all organisms and societies within that system were credited with their own internal, functional system of knowledge; and, to this extent, the Enlightenment was also relativistic. But the vision as a whole was treated quite un-relativistically: a uniquely valid vision contained, within itself, an expectation of so to speak locally functional and thus only *relatively* valid systems.

The mainstream of the Enlightenment did not properly come to terms with the tension between its naturalistic, relativist view of everything within the world, and its privileged perception of itself. It was Kant's achievement that he did fully face this contradiction. It was Weber's achievement to spell out the historical context of this tension. This contradiction was not so to speak accidental, a by-product of mere careless thought: it was deeply inherent in the logic of the situation. The lesser expositors of the Enlightenment, those salon Public Relations Offices of *lumières*, could not quite cope with this problem, and tended to ignore or evade it. Kant, as the deepest thinker of the Enlightenment, was very clear about it. Everything inside Nature was indeed subject to its laws, but knowledge itself – and morality – were *outside* it. (A fortiori, they were outside and above culture, as yet unnamed.)

Kant saw with great lucidity that *inside* Nature, conceived as an orderly system subject to laws, there was no room for a universal and unique Reason: there was room only for causation. Applied to the higher forms of life, this in effect meant the cognitive adaptation of each organism or each culture. But Nature, as a unique orderly system, was the construction, precisely, of a Reason determined to treat all like cases alike, to subsume all phenomena to an orderly system of explanation.

The result of these considerations was the stressful Kantian dualism, which consigns everything within nature (including man as an observable phenomenon) to causality and hence, by implication, when this is applied to cultures, to relativism; but it exempts us, as moral and cognizing agents, from being members of Nature, and allows us to have access to uniquely valid knowledge and morality. In a sense we created the world, which is but the shadow of our rationality; and for this very reason we neither can nor need be parts of it. We cannot *observe* ourselves as rational agents, in Kant's version of the argument, but we can infer the existence of ourselves as rational agents precisely from our capacity to experience conceptual and moral obligation. A tidy law-bound natural world, *and* a tidy law-oriented morality, were our own creation, and constitute the conclusive evidence that our true selves stood outside the Nature which they had made. For Kant, as later for Durkheim, the roots of conceptual and moral compulsion were the same. In Weber's version of the argument, an attempt is made to observe the historical emergence of that transcendence of past cultures.

Kant's ethics are reducible to the obligation to be rational, where rationality is, in essence, conceptual *orderliness*, the refusal to make exceptions (e.g. for cognitive claims), the determination to treat like cases alike (whether in moral choice or in cognitive explanation), and to unify them, as far as possible, in an orderly system. Kant's ethics apply to cognition as much as to conduct, and they are, in fact, rather more persuasive in the field of knowledge. In exploring the world, all data, all

83

information, all occasions, are to be treated alike: there are no privileged sources of illumination. The essence of sin is the making of exceptions. In other words, there is no and can be no Revelation.

This, in a nutshell, is the real cognitive ethic of the Enlightenment. It requires the breakup of data into their constituent parts, and their *impartial* confrontation with any candidate explanatory theories. It shares with monotheistic exclusive scriptural religion the belief in the existence of a unique truth, instead of an endless plurality of meaning-systems; but it repudiates the idea that this unique vision is related to a privileged Source, and could even be definitive. It shares with hermeneutic relativism the repudiation of the claim that a *substantive*, final and definitive version of the truth is available. It is, however, separated from it by refusing to endorse, as equally valid, each pre-Enlightenment, socially enmeshed, cognitive cocoon of meanings. Only a *procedure*, but no substantive ideas, is absolutized. What this now means in terms of social and political attitudes remains to be considered.

These, then, are the three principal options available in our intellectual climate: religious fundamentalism, relativism, and Enlightenment rationalism. What are their merits and defects, as systems of ideas which make claims on our allegiance?

Consider religious fundamentalism first. It unquestionably gives psychic satisfaction to many. For reasons which I have attempted to explore, it is at present quite specially persuasive and influential within one particular tradition, namely Islam. What is its weakness?

To those of us who have deeply internalized what I called the Kantian or Enlightenment ethic of cognition, the obligation to treat all evidence impartially, and all occasions as equally unprivileged, the notion of a Revelation is morally unacceptable. The idea of a unique and final Message, delivered at one place and one time, exempt from scrutiny, from the disaggregation into its constituent claims, and from the need to subject those claims to question – this violates the rules of that cognitive ethic which, for those of us who have become committed to it, constitutes the fixed point in our world-view, and the only one.

It is not so much that we necessarily quarrel with any particular part of the Message, though we may do so; and it is not the case that we are firmly, as it were religiously, wedded to any contrary and alternative substantive conviction, to the view that the world is *thus* or *thus*. We have no such fixed and firm anchorage in the world. The only such anchorage we do have, for reasons which are difficult to sustain and which I have tried to explore elsewhere,[61] is that there is in the end but one genuinely valid style of knowledge, and that, in very rough outline, the mainstream of the Western epistemological tradition, currently so unfashionable, *has* captured it. No doubt we shall be abused as positivists or worse for saying so, but there it is.

Logically, the religious fundamentalists are of course also in conflict with the relativists, who would devalue their faith with its claim to a unique revelation, and reduce it to merely one of many and equally valid 'systems of meaning'. In practice, this confrontation is not so very much in evidence. The fundamentalists notice and despise the lukewarmness and relativism so pervasive in Western society, but they do not take much interest in their philosophical rationale. The relativists in turn direct their attack only at those they castigate as 'positivists', i.e. non-relativists within their own Enlightened tradition, but play down the disagreement which logically separates them from religious fundamentalism. Their attitude is, roughly, that absolutism is to be tolerated, if only it is sufficiently alien culturally. It is only at home that they do not put up with it.

One objection to the relativists, and in particular to the hermeneutic variety of that position which we have briefly explored, is that it is deeply incoherent and, no doubt unconsciously, hypocritical. The hermeneutic relativists do not *really* treat all cultural visions as equally valid. Their accounts of alien systems of meanings as they present them are still, deeply and inevitably, located within a natural milieu conceived in terms of current Western science. Even a postmodernist anthropologist does not give an account of, for example, magical practices in a given society by saying simply, well, yes, in that culture, magic does work. He merely describes how 'it works', i.e. how that system of ideas fits into the wider web of notions and practices, seen as functioning within a Nature which itself works in the same way everywhere.

What of the weaknesses of Enlightenment rationalism (the nearest thing to a 'belief' that I can claim)?

It has a number of weaknesses, from the viewpoint of its use as a practical faith, as the foundation either for an individual life or for a social order. It is too thin and ethereal to sustain an individual in crisis, and it is too abstract to be intelligible to any but intellectuals with a penchant for this kind of theorizing. Intellectually it is all but inaccessible, and unable to offer real succour in a crisis . . . In practice, Western intellectuals, when facing personal predicaments, have turned to emotionally richer methods, offering promises of personal recovery, such as psychoanalysis.

At the social and political level, does the arid, abstract message of the Enlightenment fare any better? In fact, it had tried to do better. The creed of the Enlightenment *philosophes* was a kind of social programme, a vision of a rational order on earth which would also be a happy one. When the French *ancien régime* collapsed, this vision was waiting in the wings, and the Revolution gave it its chance. It ended, not in the reign of Reason and Nature, but first in the Terror and then in the Napoleonic dictatorship.

What had gone wrong? The nineteenth century had plenty of time to ponder this question. The most elaborate, and for a long time the most influential answer, was provided by Marxism. The answer ran: it is useless to try to establish the reign of virtue on earth by excogitating its principles and then simply applying them, as the thinkers of the Enlightenment appeared to be doing. Human society does not work like that. (In this, Marx heartily agreed with the conservative critics of the Enlightenment and of the French Revolution, from whom in fact he had learnt a great deal.) What is necessary is to understand the laws of the development of human society, the principles governing the forms and constraints actually

operative, and then to work for the liberation and final fulfilment of man, and the establishment of a rational and fulfilling
social order on earth, in the light of those principles and in
accordance with them. Happily, Marx claimed, he was in possession of those principles, and they were even such as to
guarantee a satisfactory final outcome. The social impediments
to our ultimate fulfilment were inherently 'contradictory' and,
in the end, self-destroying. When they had destroyed themselves, liberated humanity would remain as the residual
legatee.

In the twentieth century, this more sociological, sophisticated attempt to implement the Enlightenment ideal came to
be tried out. It too ended in Terror and dictatorship, and,
subsequently, in dismal economic failure and squalor into the
bargain. That experiment reached its final end in 1989, two
hundred years after the French Revolution.

What is relevant for our purposes is not so much the failure
of specific features of this particular vision – the abolition of
private property, which in the context of advanced industrialism leads to a total centralization of society, and which turns
out to be technically disastrous – features which, on their own,
could be avoided or corrected or replaced; what *is* relevant is
something broader and more generic, a weakness liable to
strike *any* attempt to extract a concrete, definite social order
from the overall vision of the Enlightenment.

The thinkers of the Enlightenment had supposed otherwise:
if religion and superstition had engendered *one* social order,
namely the hierarchical authoritarianism and dogmatism pre-
sided over by nobility and clergy, why then the true doctrine
would equally define a different, and of course much superior,
social order. An American historian has called this the Heavenly City of the Eighteenth-Century Philosophers.[62] If error
defined and legitimated one regime, then surely truth would
do as much for another, and would not this second product
be a much better one? Illusion had created, or vindicated, an
oppressive and exploitative regime; truth would engender and
satisfy a free, fraternal and egalitarian one.

But whereas error can define a society, truth cannot. Truth

does indeed corrode the old coherent visions, but fails to replace them with anything permanent, concrete, rounded-off, and morally sustaining. The valid style of inquiry generates neither stability nor normative authority. The Enlightenment ethic of cognition does exclude certain kinds of authority, certain ways of validating a social order, but it simply does not contain any solid, so to speak meaty, premisses, capable of engendering a concrete social alternative. The contrary supposition that it could do so was at the heart of the Marxist vision, and it was mistaken. So?

The viable, stable post-Enlightenment, industrial-scientific societies have so far been not those which attempted to apply a Luminous Alternative, but those which muddled through with an incoherent compromise. Marxism was not the only attempt to implement a secular religion. Nazism had less of a coherent and doctrinally codified position, but its central idea or inspiration was nevertheless clear: it was a blend of biologism and communalism. The fact that man was part of nature was to be taken seriously: he found his fulfilment in community, hierarchy, assertion. These satisfied our deepest drives. Our identity is in our earthly drives, not in anaemic ideals. Excellence precluded compassion. Though it repudiated the humanitarian and egalitarian element in the Enlightenment, in another sense, Nazism was also its continuation and fulfilment: it took with utmost seriousness the incorporation of man in Nature, and the exclusion of the transcendent from social legitimation. Men find fulfilment in assertion and community. It is our *group* that matters, and it happens to be, they claimed, the biological group. Man as an assertive and gregarious animal provides the key premiss for a new ethic. Nazism was refuted in trial by combat, just as Marxism was refuted in trial by economic growth: there is an irony in the fact that each of these secular religions found its defeat on the very ground it had itself chosen for the Final Judgement.

The elimination of these particular secular counter-faiths does not perhaps entail, though it does rather strongly suggest, that no secular salvation theory is available for mankind. We cannot actually be absolutely sure that there is no secular blueprint available which would carry conviction and work well, though the fate of the two specimens tried in the twentieth century will probably persuade many that this path is closed. But even if some such path exists and is viable, what does seem certain is that it is not uniquely prescribed by the secular view of knowledge. At best, it is rendered possible, it cannot be mandatory. So?

The linkage between ideology and political order has gone through a number of historic stages. There was first of all the pre-Axial stage in which religion was, basically, the dancing-out of the social order, the choreography of social relationships, highlighting them and legitimating them. The verbal accompaniment were but stories, not doctrines or arguments, and there could be neither disputation nor heresy. The ritual legitimation and the social order formed one barely divisible whole, and the legitimating belief system – it could barely be called such – had no pretensions either to an independent existence or to universal validity. There was no doctrinal imperialism, so to speak – if only because there was hardly any doctrine. Quite the reverse: there was a kind of deliberate isolationism. Access to the rites was restricted. Privileged and restricted entry, rather than proselytism, was the rule.

With the Axial Age, all this changed. With literacy and greater urbanization and political centralization, presumably, populations torn out of their social niches were tempted by offers of omnibus, all-purpose and all-comer salvation: universalist religions, offering total salvation, not specific assistance, were born. They were transmitted by doctrine rather than ritual, incarnated in scripture rather than sacred performance.

These religions still, however, tended to combine communal and universalistic-doctrinal, individualist elements. 'Protestant'-type tendencies were common amongst them, impelling them towards scripturalism and individualism, eliminating organized mediation, stressing a direct relationship between the individual and Truth. Generally speaking, such Reformations were not permanently successful: communal elements reasserted themselves, responding to deep social needs.

On one occasion and within one particular tradition, however, one special Reformation was much more successful than the others, and transformed the north-western corner of one continent sufficiently to help engender an industrial-scientific civilization. The Enlightenment was the reaction to this success, above all amongst its less successful and envious fringes; it strove to understand the economic and social success of the first modern societies, and make possible their emulation, and so proposed a secular version of a salvation religion, a naturalistic doctrine of universally valid salvation, in which reason and nature replaced revelation. It did so because it perceived the role of new, secular knowledge in the new social order.

The attempt to implement politically this new secular faith failed, twice over; this is the story of the aftermath of both the French and the Russian Revolutions, the two great attempts to implement the Enlightenment, to use it as the major premiss in an enormous political practical syllogism. The Bolsheviks also possessed, in Marxism, an elaborate minor premiss, in the form of a sociology of world history; it was meant to explain both why the attempt had failed the first time round, and why it would succeed under their own leadership. In the event, their attempt also failed abysmally, exactly two hundred years after the original irruption of the Enlightenment into political practice. It failed even more lamentably than had the original attempt.

What's to be done? *Shto dyelat*? We simply cannot return to the claustrophobic, isolationist relativism which our romantics recommend so blithely: each community back to its own totem pole! For one thing, we have no clearly demarcated communities; the ones we have are fluid and unstable. Real knowledge is not linked to any one totem pole, but free of them all, and we are dependent on it and cannot really abjure it, even if some of us rather comically pretend to do so. Hermeneutic relativism provides a philosophic rationale which is not merely logically absurd (that in itself wouldn't matter too much), but it also commends something that is socially unviable.

Can we, then follow the fundamentalists of the scripturalist world religions? Their recipe does seem viable, at any rate within one of the existing world religions. But such a solution, whether or not it can be exported from the area where it seems to be prevailing for the time being, is unacceptable to us liberals who are also the heirs of the Enlightenment. Within at least one of the world civilizations, the liberals seem strong enough, numerous enough and well established enough to resist any such attempt. What, then, should be the new relation between faith and social order?

The attractive solution, it seems to me, is what might be called constitutional religion, on the analogy of constitutional monarchy (an institution which works fairly well in a certain number of polities). What *is* constitutional monarchy in effect? It is a system which retains the ritual and symbolism of genuine monarchy, whilst transferring most of the real business of running society to a more technical, secular and unsacralized sphere. On the assumption that ritual theatre is needed, but that the 'new science' either cannot produce it, or will only produce a disastrous version, the ritual and the real spheres of social life become separated. Ritual now mirrors, not the real situation, but the past or a fictitious distribution of social power. The separation of powers is extended to the institutionalization of the distinction between symbolism and decision-making. Ritual reflects not social reality but social phantasy, but contributes to social stability by not endowing temporary and technical centres of power with any sacred aura, and not imperilling them by linking their legitimacy to doctrines which may be proved false tomorrow. This disconnectedness seems to work rather well.

So constitutional monarchies seem to function satisfactorily. But the point of the present argument is not to commend this principle in the sphere of political symbolism, but to make explicit the nature of its applicability in the wider and more general sphere of the relationship of belief and practice. We live in a post-Enlightenment world, in a very precise sense: the idea that a secular version of Revelation is available and will supply the blueprint of an attractive and legitimate social order is rightly in disrepute. Its failures have been too conspicuous and too horrible. But, at the same time, the Enlightenment

91

has codified the only seriously acceptable principles of valid knowledge. The fashionable relativistic denials of those principles are logically absurd, and distasteful morally; they can only be embraced as affectations, even if those who embrace them are not properly aware of this. When dealing with serious matters, when human lives and welfare are at stake, when major resources are being committed, the only kind of knowledge which may legitimately be used and invoked is that which satisfies the criteria of Enlightenment philosophy – notwithstanding the fact that it is not easy to formulate these with precision or to general satisfaction, and that it may be impossible to demonstrate their authority.

The viable compromise, the equivalent of constitutional monarchy in the sphere of conviction, is a kind of double authority, with the separation of their respective zones left deliberately obscure and ambiguous. In the sphere of legitimation of social arrangements, the old pieties are retained in the social liturgy; in the sphere of serious cognition, they are ignored. The cultural Broad Church which embraces them both allows individuals to locate themselves at will along this spectrum, and in no way obliges or expects them to be consistent in their self-location: they can move sideways according to context, occasion or mood.

One of the first persons to face this problem was David Hume. In his main work on religion, *Natural History of Religion*, he operates in terms of a distinction corresponding to our contrast between fundamentalism and relativism. His tolerant temper tends him to favour relativism, in the form in which it was and could still be implemented in the classical world, prior to the coming of doctrinal and scriptural religion. The old traditional religions were tolerant of each other, civic, communal, this-worldly, and were replaced by scripturalist doctrines claiming universal applicability and given to hunting the heretic. Freedom, Hume noted, stood a better chance with the priests attending to the ancient rites, than the puritans obsessed with doctrine. But lo and behold – and Hume notices this both in his essay on 'Superstition and Enthusiasm', and in his *History of Great Britain* – in the modern world, freedom fared better under the doctrine-obsessed puritans than under the priests!

The enthusiasm of the puritans is, after all, more freedom-friendly than superstition of the ancients. How can this be? This goes against the logic of his main argument, but he has the honesty to notice it and worry about it. He finds a half-satisfactory answer in terms of what Max Weber was later to call 'routinization'.

Hume's solution need not detain us. What is important is that he saw and clearly formulated the problem. The explanation seems to be that the 'enthusiast' puritans, defeated but not crushed, opted for toleration and came to terms with the *ancien régime*, and turned to commerce; their zeal, aided eventually by a new technology born of the science to which they also contributed, sanctified the compromise by widespread prosperity, and a society in which lukewarm faith and unstable, growing secular knowledge co-exist under 'constitutional religion', as I have called it, came into being. It is relativistic in its symbolism and what might be called 'legitimative' quasi-doctrine, but absolutist in its serious pursuit of earthly truth. This seems to be the acceptable political theory which is to accompany rationalist absolutism (rather than a mundane counter-revelation, exemplified most clearly by Marxism).

No doubt, this kind of constitutional arrangement is open to some criticisms. Quite probably, the break-through to the 'scientific miracle' was only possible because some men were passionately, sincerely, whole-heartedly concerned with truth. Will such passion survive the habit of granting oneself different kinds of truth according to the day of the week? Conversely, societies have faced major crises with the help of genuine social conviction; can they do so with the help of an ironic, non-serious faith, disconnected from genuine conviction about how things truly stand? My guess, as well as my hope, is that both questions can be given at least a tentative affirmative answer: genuine, socially disconnected inquiry into the nature of the world, once it is as well institutionalized as it is, and once it is known to be so effective, can probably survive even a more opportunistic, un-rigorous, un-protestant frame of mind; and the overcoming of social crises is perhaps hampered as much as assisted by excessive faith. Pragmatic goodwill may be sufficient. This is a reasonable hope, though it would be idle to pretend that one can in any way guarantee such an optimism. We cannot do any better.[63]

The coherent secular counter-visions have proved disastrous in practice. The successful societies which use – but do not formally sacralize – the new secular knowledge are those based on compromise. They continue to use a pre-industrial idiom of social legitimation, but treat it with limited seriousness and do not allow it to interfere with serious cognitive and productive business. They equally refrain from taking too seriously any of the ideological spin-offs of the 'new knowledge', which purport to offer a new, secular, 'scientific' salvation. They live like a man who takes the plumbing, lighting and structure of his home from modern technology, but all of whose furnishing and decoration is strictly *period*. That way, he can be warm and comfortable, and at the same time satisfy his taste for aesthetic coherence, at least on the surface. Max Weber was somewhat contemptuous of the underlying incoherence of such an attitude, but I do not see that we can do any better.

The mild rationalist fundamentalism which is being commended does not attempt, as the Enlightenment did, to offer a rival counter-model to its religious predecessor. It is fundamentalist only in connection with the form of knowledge, and perhaps in the form of morality, insisting on symmetry of treatment for all. (I hesitate at this point: in the sphere of knowledge, rational symmetry is pragmatically underwritten, so to speak enforced, by its practical success and power. This does not apply in morality. At present, a mobile occupational structure, itself a corollary of economic growth, makes a certain formal baseline egalitarianism and the ethic of symmetrical treatment which goes with it widely popular – but I wonder whether this will survive a restabilization of the occupational structure, if that ever comes.) Otherwise, on all points of detail and content, it compromises. This, if you like, is its concession to nihilism, its similarity to relativism. Where no good reasons are available one can go along with the contingencies of local development, the accidents of local balance of power and taste. Serious knowledge is not subject to relativism, but the trappings of our cultural life are.

The relativists, in whatever guise – the 'postmodernists' are but an extravagant, undisciplined and transient mode of this attitude – seem to me to offer an accurate and acceptable account of how we do, and probably of how we should, order our gastronomy (at any rate on any one evening), our wallpaper, and even, for lack of a better alternative, our daily self-image. (Though most evenings, I'd prefer a traditional rather than postmodernist menu.) Their insights apply to the decorative rather than the real structural and functional aspects of our life. When they try to apply their insights too far, they constitute a preposterous travesty of the real role of serious knowledge in our lives, and even, for what it is worth, of the actual practice of social science. Societies are systems of real constraints, operating in a unique nature, and must be understood as such, and not simply as systems of meaning – even if compulsive meanings do play their (rather variable) role. To pretend otherwise is not merely error but also self-deception. It is error which is in blatant conflict with what, in other contexts, we know perfectly well. It is self-delusion.

The fundamentalists deserve our respect, both as fellow recognizers of the uniqueness of truth, who avoid the facile self-deception of universal relativism, and as our intellectual ancestors. Without indulging in excessive ancestor-worship, we do owe them a measure of reverence. Without serious, not to say obsessional monotheism and unitarianism, the rationalist naturalism of the Enlightenment might well never have seen the light of day. In all probability, the attachment to a unique Revelation was the historical pre-condition of the successful emergence of a unique and symmetrically accessible Nature. It was a jealous Jehovah who really taught mankind the Law of the Excluded Middle: Greek formalization of logic (and geometry and grammar) probably would not have been sufficient on its own. Without a strong religious impulsion towards a single orderly world, and the consequent avoidance of opportunist, manipulative incoherence, the cognitive miracle would probably not have occurred.

This respect, however, does not oblige us to obscure our disagreements with the fundamentalists. In fact, the respect for truth we inherited from them would be untrue to itself if it were to hide them. The notion of a Revelation favouring and endorsing its own source, reconfirming itself by a blatantly circular argument, is incompatible with that very cognitive ethic which, for all its emotional thinness, I find at the centre of my identity. Of course one welcomes those fundamentalist believers who convey their willingness to compromise by an eagerness for 'dialogue'; viable social systems hinge on such compromise. One's respect for the seriousness of the fundamentalists' attitude to truth, one's gratitude for tolerance, compete with one's objection to the content of their conviction. A jealous God taught us to think symmetrically; and what this has taught us prevents us from accepting any claims to Revelation.

To the relativists, one can only say – you provide an excellent account of the manner in which we choose our menu or our wallpaper. As an account of the realities of our world and a guide to conduct, your position is laughable. Possibly you may be doing good by encouraging political compromise. If the ambiguities of your formulations and attitude help ease the situation, and bring forth a compromise between the believers and the others, or between rival believers, you may yet be performing a public service.

Ernest Gellner
July 1991

NOTES

1 S. Kierkegaard, *Kierkegaard's Concept of Dread*, trans. Walter Lowrie, London: Humphrey Milford, Oxford University Press, 1944.
2 W. Herberg, *Protestant-Catholic-Jew: An Essay in American Religious Sociology*, new edn, Garden City, NY: Anchor Books and Doubleday, 1960.
3 D. Martin, *A General Theory of Secularization*, Oxford: Blackwell, 1978.
4 E. Gellner, *Muslim Society*, Cambridge: Cambridge University Press, 1981.
5 W. W. Bartley, *The Retreat to Commitment*, London: Chatto & Windus, 1964.
6 M. A. Cook, *Muhammad*, Oxford: Oxford University Press, 1983.
7 Cf. N. R. Keddie (ed.), *Scholars, Saints and Sufis*, Berkeley, CA: University of California Press, 1972.
8 Ibn Khaldun, *Muqaddima*, trans. F. Rosenthal, London: Routledge & Kegan Paul, 1958.
9 P. Crone and M. Hinds, *God's Caliph: Religious Authority in the First Centuries of Islam*, Cambridge: Cambridge University Press, 1986.
10 Cf. H. Laoust, *Les Schismes dans l'Islam*, Paris: Payot, 1965.
11 Ibn Khaldun, *Muqaddima*.
12 D. Hume, 'The Natural History of Religion', in *Hume on Religion*, ed. R. Wollheim, London: Collins, 1963.
13 F. Engels, 'Contribution to the history of Christianity', in *Die Neue Zeit*, quoted in R. Gallissot and G. Badia (eds), *Marxisme et Algérie*, Paris: Collection, 10/18, UGE, 1976.
14 E. Loone, *Sovremennaya Filosofiya Istorii*, Tallin: Eesti Raamat, 1980, to be published in English as *Soviet Marxism and Analytical Philosophies of History*, London: Verso, 1992.
15 B. Turner, *Weber and Islam: A Critical Study*, London: Routledge & Kegan Paul, 1974.
16 V. Maher, *Women and Property in Morocco: Their Changing Relation*

to the Process of Social Stratification in the Middle Atlas, Cambridge: Cambridge University Press, 1974.

17 R. Danziger, *Abd al-Qadir and the Algerians: Resistance to the French and Internal Consolidation*, New York: Holmes & Meier, 1977.

18 E. Durkheim, *The Elementary Forms of the Religious Life*, trans. J. W. Swain, London: George Allen & Unwin, 1915 (1971).

19 Cf. H. Munson, Jr, *Islam and Revolution in the Middle East*, New Haven, CT, and London: Yale University Press, 1988.

20 'Ayat' Allah Khumayni, *Islam and Revolution: Writings and Declarations of Imam Khomeni*, trans. Hamid Algar, Berkeley, CA: Mizan Press, 1981.

21 Said Amir Arjomand, *The Shadow of God and the Hidden Imam: Religion, Political Order and Societal Change in Shi'ite Iran from the Beginning to 1890*, Chicago, IL: University of Chicago Press, 1984.

22 'Ayat' Allah Khumayni, *Islam and Revolution*.

23 M. Weber, *The Protestant Ethic and the Spirit of Capitalism*, trans. Talcott Parsons, New York: Allen & Unwin, 1930 (1950).

24 See J. Spencer, 'Anthropology as a kind of writing', *Man*, n.s., vol. 24, March 1989, pp. 145–64.

25 R. Fardon, 'Malinowski's precedent: the imagination of equality', *Man*, vol. 25, no. 4, December 1990, pp. 569–71.

26 J. G. Merquior, *The Veil and the Mask: Essays on Culture and Ideology*, London: Routledge & Kegan Paul, 1979.

27 P. Rabinow in J. Clifford and G. E. Marcus (eds), *Writing Culture: The Poetics and Politics of Ethnography*, Berkeley, CA: University of California Press, 1986.

28 Ibid., p. 245.

29 Ibid., p. 246.

30 Ibid., pp. 248 and 249.

31 T. Adorno *et al.*, *The Positivist Dispute in German Sociology*, trans. G. Ades and D. Frisby, London: Heinemann Educational Books, 1976.

32 H. Marcuse, *One-Dimensional Man*, London: Routledge & Kegan Paul, 1964.

33 T. Adorno *et al.*, *The Positivist Dispute in German Sociology*.

34 See for instance Clifford and Marcus, *Writing Culture*, p. 132.

35 An extreme version of liberation from epistemological critique is the anarchism of P. Feyerabend, *Against Method: Outline of an Anarchistic Theory of Knowledge*, London: Verso, 1979.

36 Rabinow, p. 236.

37 Ibid., p. 241.

38 Ibid., p. 252.

39 Ibid., p. 25.

40 G. E. Marcus, 'Ethnography in the modern world system', in ibid., p. 167.

NOTES

41 C. Geertz, *Works and Lives: The Anthropologist as Author*, Cambridge: Polity, 1988, pp. 59; 70 and 71.
42 Ibid., p. 71.
43 Rabinow, p. 253.
44 N. Barley, *The Innocent Anthropologist: Notes from a Mud Hut*, London: British Museum Publications, 1983; and *Not a Hazardous Sport*, London: Viking, 1988.
45 Marcus, 'Ethnography in the modern world system', p. 169.
46 Rabinow, p. 252.
47 C. Geertz, 'Anti anti relativism', *American Anthropologist*, 1984, pp. 263–78.
48 I. C. Jarvie, 'Rationality and relativism', *The British Journal of Sociology*, vol. 34, no. 1, March 1983, pp. 44–60.
49 Geertz, 'Anti anti relativism'.
50 Ibid.
51 Ibid., p. 276, fn. 2.
52 London: Routledge, 1945 (1966), vols I and II.
53 K. R. Popper, *Objective Knowledge: An Evolutionary Approach*, Oxford: Clarendon Press, 1972, p. 261.
54 Geertz, 'Anti anti relativism', p. 264.
55 K. Jaspers, *Vom Ursprung und Ziel der Geschichte*, Munich: Piper Verlag, 1949, pp. 15–106.
56 S. N. Eisenstadt (ed.), *The Origins and Diversity of Axial Age Civilizations*, Albany, NY: State University of New York Press, 1986.
57 Geertz, 'Anti anti relativism'.
58 C. Geertz, *Negara: The Theatre State of 19th Century Bali*, Princeton, NJ: Princeton University Press, 1980.
59 Rabinow, p. 253.
60 Baron d'Holbach (P.H.D. Holbach), *The System of Nature, or Laws of the Moral and Physical World*, trans. H. D. Robinson, New York: Lenox Hill (Burt Franklin), 1970.
61 E. Gellner, *Legitimation of Belief*, London: Cambridge University Press, 1974.
62 C. L. Becker, *Heavenly City of the Eighteenth Century Philosophers*, New Haven, CT: Yale University Press, 1932.
63 Max Weber, *Science as a Vocation*, ed. P. Lassman and I. Velody, London: Unwin Hyman, 1989.

INDEX

Abd el Kader, 13
Abd el Krim, 13
absolutism: Marxist, 31; of
  procedural principles of
  knowledge, 80–4, 93; relativists
  and, 73, 74, 84, 85; religious,
  80
Adorno, T., 33
affluence and religious faith, 22,
  93
Algeria, 12, 13
American Anthropologist, 49
Amerindians, 65
anthropological theory:
  postmodernism and, 23, 26,
  27, 70
anthropology: use of interpretive
  techniques in, 68; hermeneutic
  see hermeneutics, hermeneutic
  anthropology; influence of
  postmodernism on *see*
  postmodernism; social versus
  cultural, 65–6; *see also* fieldwork
apostasy, 74, 75
Arabia, 13
astro-physics, 4
astrology, 6
author, author-inquirer, 25, 28,
  29; plural, 28; *see also* observer
authority, 58; double, of new
  relationship between faith and

social order, 92; Enlightenment
  and, 87–8

Balinese state, 69
Becker, C. L., 87
binary oppositions, 1, 23, 35
biologism, 88
Bolsheviks, 90

Caliphate, 9
Caucasus, 13
China: religion, 6
Christianity, 17; doctrine, 6 *see
  also* doctrine; and political
  struggle, 10
clarity, ethnographic *see under*
  ethnography
class: Marxist theory, 10–11, 31,
  32–3; in post-colonial state, 65
classicism, 26
Clifford, James, 28, 38, 40, 43
coercion as social constraint, 63–4
cognitive relativism and
  asymmetry, 37–8, 55–6, 61–2,
  69, 70, 71, 78–9; *see also*
  knowledge, theory of
cognitive subjectivity, 27, 35–6
colonialism, 26, 30, 36, 43, 44, 47,
  48, 57, 66; Islam and, 15, 21;
  see also domination

commerce, 22, 93; *see also* industrialism; technology
commitment, religion as, 3
communalism, 88
communication, 42, 45
Communism *see* Marxism
communities: instability of modern, 90; multiplicity of, 57; *see also* cultures
community: faith and celebration of, 3, 4–5
compromise, 94, 96
conceptual constraints in society, 63–4
conflicts, intellectual, 1
Congress of the CPSU(B), XXth, 32
constitutional monarchy, 91, 92
constitutional religion as new relation between faith and social order, 91–4
context, 68
counter-organization: Church as, 5
critical theory *see* Frankfurt School
cultural diversity: American failure to appreciate *see* provincialism
cultural equality, 47, 48, 49–50, 60, 63, 73–4, 85–6; *see also* relativism
cultural inequality in Western philosophy, 37–8
cultural meaning *see* meaning(s)
culture, understanding of, 62
cultures: equality, inequality of *see* cultural; folk, 26; instability of, 71; traditional, 78, 80, 89; *see also* communities
Cyrenaica, 13

Darwinism, 4
decolonization, 26, 66; *see also* colonialism
deconstruction, 23, 36, 40

Descartes, René, 30, 37–8
dialogic presentation, 27–8
discourse, 63
dissidence: Marxism and, 31
diversity, cultural: American failure to appreciate *see* provincialism
doctrine, 2, 3, 4, 5, 6, 57, 89, 92; Islamic *see under* Islam
domination: British, and anthropology, 43–4; clarity and objectivity in ethnography related to, 26, 27, 30, 36, 39, 41, 45–6, 67, 73; meaning and, 24; political, 58–9, 61, 63–4; postwar American, 42–3, 45; *see also* colonialism; decolonization
Durkheim, E., Durkheimian sociology, 14, 83

Eastern Europe: events of 1989, 60, 87, 90
economic constraints in society, 63
economic growth, 94
economy: relation to beliefs and culture, 21–2
egalitarianism, 52, 94; Enlightenment, 88; and hermeneutic anthropology, 30, 47, 48, 56–7, 60, 62–3, 73–4, 85–6; Islamic, 17
Einstein, A., 51
Eisenstadt, S. N., 57
elections, 16
empiricism, 36, 81
Engels, Friedrich, 10–11, 13
England *see* Great Britain
Enlightenment: cognitive theory, 58, 76, 80, 82–4, 87–8, 90, 91–2, 94, 95; and social order, 7, 90
Enlightenment rationalism *see* rationalist fundamentalism
epistemology *see* knowledge, theory of

equality *see* egalitarianism

ethnocentrism *see* provincialism

ethnography: clarity related to domination, 26, 27, 28, 30, 43–4, 45, 67, 68; experimentation, 42–3; interpretive *see* hermeneutics, hermeneutic anthropology; postmodern *see* postmodernism

Evans-Pritchard, Edward, 43–4, 68

existentialism, 3

facts *see* objective reality, objective truth

faith: fundamental positions, 1–2; new relationship between social order and, 91–6; *see also* modernism, religious; religious fundamentalism

Fardon, R., 25, 35

feminist movement, 27

festivals *see* ritual

fieldwork, 36, 44, 45, 46–7; difficulties of post-colonial, 65–6

folk cultures, 26

Folk Islam *see under* Islam

folk religion, 6; Islamic *see under* Islam

Foucault, M., 39

France, 14, 19, 26; Revolution, 86, 87

Frankfurt School, 32–5, 37

Franklin, Benjamin, 52

freedom, 27, 30, 48, 51, 52, 92–3

Geertz, Clifford, 40, 43–5, 48, 49–54, 55, 60, 64, 68, 69

gender, 27

generalization, anthropological *see* anthropological theory

Genesis, Book of, 4

Germany, 19; links between philosophical idealism and academic life, 48; society, 64

Giddens, Anthony, 47

Great Britain: links between anthropology and imperialism, 43–4; science and industrialism, 61; society, 52

Greek thought, 9, 57, 95

Hegel, G. W. F., Hegelian philosophy, 31, 64

Heidegger, M., 37

Heine, Heinrich, 48

hermeneutic truth, 35

hermeneutics, hermeneutic anthropology, 24, 25, 26, 29, 30, 36, 37, 38, 46, 47, 52, 55, 56, 62–8, 71, 74, 85, 90; Geertz's, 40, 43–5, 48; *see also* relativism

heteroglossic presentation, 27–8

High Islam *see under* Islam

Hume, David, 10, 37, 78, 92

Ibn Khaldun, 10, 13

idealism, 31, 63, 64, 66

ideas as social constraints, 63–4

identity: linked to faith, 3; postmodernism and, 29

imperialism *see* colonialism

Indian World: religion, 6

individualism, 52, 89

industrialism, industrialized society, 22, 61, 79, 87, 88, 90

informant, 28–9, 36, 65

innovation, 52

'intégrisme' *see* religious fundamentalism

interpretive anthropology *see* hermeneutics, hermeneutic anthropology

interpretive techniques: anthropologist's use of, 68

Iranian revolution, 16–18

Islam, 4, 5, 6–22, 72–3, 84; doctrine, 6–7, 11, 17, 72–3; ecstasy, 11, 12; High Islam, 9, 10–14, 15, 17, 19–21, 72;

history, 9; influence of technology on, 14; Iranian revolution, 16–18; law and morality, 6–7, 8, 9, 17, 18; Low or Folk Islam, 9, 10–14, 15, 16, 17, 20–1; mediation in, 8, 11–12, 14, 16, 17–18; politics, 7–22; revivalist movements, 9–10, 13–14, 15, 17–18, 19–21, 22; sects, 6, 8, 16–18; and West, 13, 16, 19, 21, 72, 74–5, 85

Jarvie, Ian, 49
Jaspers, Karl, 57

Kant, Immanuel, Kantian rationalism, 37, 80, 81, 82–4
Kharejites, 6, 8
Khomeini, Ayatollah, 17–18
Kierkegaard, Søren, 3
Kipling, Rudyard, 30
knowledge: American organization of fields of, 42–3
knowledge, theory of, 37–40; Big Ditch theory, 50–1; empiricist theory of, 81; Kant's theory of transcendence of, 82–4; of rationalist fundamentalism, 54, 61, 75–82; and relativism, 25, 27, 35–6, 37–40, 42, 44, 45, 48, 54, 73; see also cognitive relativism and asymmetry; Enlightenment, cognitive theory; science; scientific method
Krushchev, N., 32

language, 63; of postmodernism see postmodernism, style and obscurity
law, Islamic see under Islam
Lehrer, Tom, 42
liberalism, 1, 91
liberation see freedom
linguistics see language

literacy and religious fundamentalism, 2, 11, 89; see also scripturalism
literary studies and postmodernism, 23
Low Islam see under Islam

magic, 11, 85–6
Mahdia, 13
Malinowskian anthropology, 43
Marcus, G. E., 38, 42–3, 47
Marcuse, H., 33
martyrs, Islamic, 17
Marxism, 10–11; as ancestor of postmodernism, 31–3, 34, 37; attempt to implement secular religion, 86–7, 88, 90, 93
meaning(s), 23, 24, 67, 95; Descartes and, 38; Frankfurt School and, 33; Marxism and, 31; and postmodern and hermeneutic social anthropology, 23, 26, 27, 35, 36–7, 47, 62–3, 65, 66, 67–8, 73, 74
mediation 89; in Islam see under Islam
membership, religious faith and, 3, 4–5
minorities, minority movements, 27, 65
modernism: in literature, 24, 29, 30; religious, 2–4
monotheism, 6, 11, 58, 72–3, 95
morality, 54, 55, 73, 80, 83, 94; Islamic see under Islam; and science, 59
Morocco, 12, 13
Muhammad, Prophet, 6, 8, 12, 19, 21
Muhammad Ibn 'Abd Allah, 13
multiple voices, 28
Muslim, Muslims see Islam

narcissism-hermeneuticism, 26

national state, nationalism, 4–5, 15, 21
Nature, natural science: Enlightenment theory *see* Enlightenment, cognitive theory
Nazism, 88
Nietzsche, F. W., 45, 48
Nigeria, 13
nihilism, 49–50, 53, 54, 55, 71, 95
North America: Declaration of Independence, 52; hegemony and academic life, 42–3, 45, 46; provincialism *see* provincialism; religion, 5; sociology, 46
North Yemen, 14

object, 70–1
objective reality, objective truth, 23, 25, 26, 27, 29, 31, 32, 33, 35, 37, 69–70, 75, 84; Western philosophy and, 30, 37–8
objectivity: Frankfurt School and, 33, 34, 37; Marxism and, 32–3, 37; postmodernism and hermeneuticism and, 24, 27, 28, 30, 35, 37, 41, 43, 67, 69
observer in postmodernism and hermeneuticism, 25, 26, 30, 47, 65, 69; bias, 28–9
occupational structure and egalitarianism, 94
oil and Muslim economy, 21, 22
Old World, 5–6
Osman dan Fodio, 13
Other, 23, 36, 40, 48, 56, 70, 71

Parsons, Talcott, 43
patriarchy, 30, 57
Persia, 18; *see also* Iranian revolution
pessimism, 55
philosophy, 29, 78; Greek, 9, 57, 95; influence of postmodernism on, 23; of

science, 59; *see also* knowledge, theory of
phonetics, 35
physics, 56–7
Pirandello, Luigi, 41
pluralism, 7, 74
political constraints in society, 63–4
political order: applications of Enlightenment philosophy to, 86–9, 90; Islamic, 7–22; links between religion and, 89–90; new relation between faith and, 91–6; and postmodernism, 42–8; and secularization *see* secularization, theory of
political struggle, 10
Popper, Karl, 34, 51
populism: Muslims and, 19, 20
positivism, 23, 25, 26, 33, 34, 36, 37, 47, 85
postmodernism, 2, 22–40, 66, 67, 69–70, 71, 72, 85–6, 95; as academic exercise, 27, 45–6, 48, 72; ambiguity, 27; and comprehension of alien culture, 56, 74; definition of, 29; dialogic and heteroglossic presentation, 27–8; Frankfurt School as ancestor of, 32–5, 37; and knowledge, 25, 27, 35–6, 37–40, 42, 44, 45, 48; Marxism as ancestor of, 31–2, 33, 34, 37; style and obscurity, 29, 30, 36–7, 42, 45, 56, 67, 70, 73
power: inequalities of, 42, 69; *see also* domination
pragmatism, 52, 94
private property: abolition of, 87
production, 31
prosperity and religious faith, 22, 93
provincialism, 49, 50, 51–3, 56, 60–1, 71, 74
psychoanalysis, 86

puritanism, 22, 92–3; Islamic, 11, 13, 17, 22

Rabinow, P., 28, 29, 38–41, 43, 45–6, 47, 48, 69
rationalism *see* Enlightenment, cognitive theory
rationalist fundamentalism, 2, 75–96; basic stance, 80; compared with relativism, 75–6, 80, 84, 95; compared with religious fundamentalism, 75, 80, 84; constitutional religion, 91–6; development of, 76, 82–4; weaknesses of, 86–9
reality, 30, 31; *see also* objective reality, objective truth
reason, 1, 30, 83, 90
Reformation, 90
relativism, 2, 24–72, 79, 90, 95; academic status of, 50, 74; as affectation, 70–1, 92; author's expectation of, 76–8; cognitive, 37–8, 55–6, 61–2, 69, 70, 71, 78–9; compared with rationalist fundamentalism, 75–6, 80, 84, 95; definition, 54; Enlightenment, 82, 83, 92; Geertz and, 40, 43–5, 49–54, 60, 68; greatest objections to, 62–71, 85–6; Jarvie's summary of, 49; moral *see* morality; postmodernism as form of *see* postmodernism; summary of merits, 96; tolerance, 73, 74, 84
religion: constitutional, as new relation between faith and social order, 91–4; development of, 57–8; Enlightenment and, 87; and political order, 89–90
religious fundamentalism, 2–22, 71; compared with rationalist fundamentalism, 75, 80, 84; importance for development

of rationalist fundamentalism, 95–6; Islam as example of *see* Islam; meaning of, 2–4; merits and defects, 84–5; terms, 2
republicanism of Khomeini, 18
Revelation, 76, 80, 81, 84–5, 90, 95, 96; *see also* Islam
rigorism *see* religious fundamentalism
ritual, 2, 4, 5, 21, 57, 78, 89, 91; Islamic, 10, 12, 14
romanticism, 26, 27, 70, 90
Rorty, Richard, 37, 38–9
'routinization', 93
Rushdie, Salman, 74, 75
Russell, Bertrand, 35
Russia: Revolution and society, 64, 90; Westernization and Populism/Slavophilism, 19, 20

sacred *see* Revelation
saint-cult in Islam *see* Islam, mediation in
Sanussiyya, 13
Sartre, Jean-Paul, 1, 72
science, scientific knowledge, 51, 57, 58–60, 61–2, 93; Marxists and, 32–3; religious modernism and, 4
scientific method, 80–8
scientism, 46–7
scripturalism, 78, 89, 92; Islamic, 11, 13, 17, 22; *see also* doctrine; literacy
secular faiths, 5, 6, 86–9, 90, 91, 94
secular knowledge *see* science, scientific knowledge
secularization, theory of, 4–6, 18–22
self, 36
separation of powers: in Muslim society, 7, 9; in new relationship between faith and order, 91–2
Shamil, 13

Shi'ites, Shi'ism, 6, 8, 16–18
shrines, 15, 16
social anthropology see anthropology
social change, 20, 58–60, 61; see also technology
social control, social stability, 63–4, 68, 91
social legitimation, 8, 73, 94
social order: influence of scientific knowledge on see social change; monotheism and, 73; new relationship between faith and, 91–6; religion and, 89–90
social programme of Enlightenment, 86
social sciences, 25, 27, 43; see also anthropology; sociology
social status in Reformist Islam, 15–16
social structures, 29, 47, 65–6
social theory, 47
socialism, 1
society: coercive and economic versus conceptual constraints, 63–4, 68, 71–2, 95; Marxist view of, 86–7; understanding of, 62
sociology, sociological theory, 79; American, 46, 47; Marxist, of world history, 90; see also Weber, Max
Somaliland, 13
state: Balinese, 69; post-colonial, 47, 65; see also political order
stream of consciousness, 24, 30
structuraliste movement, 35
student protest of 1960s, 32, 33
sub-cultures, 68
subject, subjectivity in postmodernism, 23, 24, 26, 28, 29, 35–6, 40–1
subject-object distinction in writing, 67
subjectivism: Frankfurt School,

33, 34; Marxist historical, 32; relativist, 27, 30, 45–6, 47
Sudan, 13
Sunnis, Sunnism, 6, 8, 16, 17
symbolic truth see truth; and religion
symbolism: hermeneutics and, 63, 66; of Islam, 11; and new relationship between faith and social order, 91

technology, technical power, 71, 75, 82, 93; influence on Islam, 14
text, 23, 25
Tocqueville, A. de, 14
toleration: of relativism, 73, 74, 84; see also freedom
transcendence of scientific method, 81–4
Transcendent and Social: relationship in history, 57, 89
tribes, tribalism, 65; Islamic, 9–10, 11–15, 18
truth; constitutional religion and, 93; Descartes and, 38; Frankfurt School and, 34; Marxism and, 31, 32; postmodernism and hermeneutic, 24, 35–6, 70; and religion, 3–4, 58, 89, 95, 96; and scientific method, 80, 87–8; see also objective reality, objective truth

under-developed countries, 18–19
unitarianism, 95
United States of America see North America
urbanization, 89; Islamic, 11, 12, 13, 15–16, 22

Wahabi movement, 13
Wars of Religion, 1
Weber, Max, Weberian

INDEX

Wesley, John, 22

West: image of East, 39; Islam and *see under* Islam

Wittgenstein, L. J. J., 24, 37, 74

women, 27, 67; Muslim, 16

work, 21, 22

writing and religious fundamentalism *see* literacy

Yemen Arab Republic, 14